Contemporary Upholstery

Techniques and Inspiration for Upstyling Your Furniture

HANNAH STANTON

jacqui
small

Contents

SECTION 2
Working With Fabrics

Contemporary Upholstery

First published in 2013 by
Jacqui Small llp
An imprint of Aurum Press
74 White Lion Street
London N1 9PF

© 2013 by RotoVision SA
www.rotovision.com

The author's moral rights have been asserted.

ISBN: 978 1 906417 91 8
A catalogue record for this book is available from the British Library.

10 9 8 7 6 5 4 3 2 1

Cover design: Emily Portnoi
Art director: Emily Portnoi
Art editor: Jennifer Osborne
Design concept: Emily Portnoi
Design and art direction (Section 1): Jennifer Osborne
Layout: Katy Abbott
Illustrations: Peters & Zabransky
Photography (pages 10–35): Michael Wicks
Editor: Liz Jones
Picture research: Diane Leyman & Hannah Stanton

Printed in China by 1010 Printing International Ltd.

SECTION 3

Upholstery Techniques

SECTION 4

Resources

Introduction

As a subscriber to all manner of design, craft and home-making blogs, it's pretty clear to me that in most of our homes there's an upholstery project waiting to happen. Whether you're taking that first daunting step, or wanting to move on to a more complex project, I hope this book will guide and inspire you.

Recycling, upcycling and revamping are not new concepts. The general maintenance of household furniture sat alongside home cooking back in the day. While there has always been a hard core of makers and crafters out there, there is now a new breed, who previously wouldn't have considered taking on such projects, but have been inspired by blogs such as *Design*Sponge* and *Apartment Therapy*. The case studies in this book showcase a selection of projects from this new generation of upholsterers.

As a teenager, I began collecting furniture, scouring the local junk shops and auction rooms – abandoning it all when I headed to London. I spent the early 1990s working in a scrap yard – the glamour! – but it was the perfect home for my hoard. Without enough cash to open that reclamation yard, the desire for a proper job kicked in and I took a degree and became a graphic designer. Screen bound and frustrated, I had no time to control the mountain of furniture building up around me. All were in various stages of undress – some just in bits. Barely able to find my husband Matthias among the wreckage, I decided to do something about it. The practical, 'need to know' gene kicked in and I joined an army of (mainly) women on a course in Traditional and Modern Upholstery, taught by the legendary Malcolm Hopkins.

Upholstery is a skill, and the more you learn, the more you realise there is to learn. The inner workings of a chair can seem daunting, but with a few basic skills coupled with a touch of common sense, you can transform that neglected wingback. Keep an eye on the style scene, experiment with materials and develop your own techniques. There is however nothing better than learning hands-on from an experienced craftsman. If this book gives you the bug – and I hope it does – find yourself one of these guys. Learn the old time skills and rules, then enjoy every minute of breaking them…

Top: Regency-style chair upholstered by Hannah Stanton in Cranes fabric from Florence Broadhurst.

Above: Deep-buttoned, iron-back Victorian nursing chair upholstered by Hannah Stanton in Jacobean at Night fabric by Celia Birtwell.

1950s chair upholstered in
Outback fabric by Kvadrat
by Hannah Stanton.

PROTEAFLORA

SECTION 1
The Basics

Fler armchairs upholstered
with Grevillea fabric by Ink & Spindle.

Ripping down tools

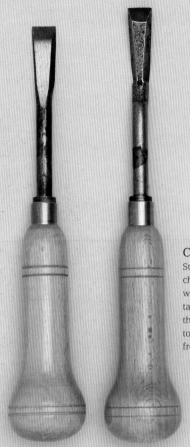

TACK LIFTER
Lifts tacks and decorative nails. Easy to use and can quickly remove temporary tacks from the frame. The end is cranked at a 45-degree angle to aid leverage.

CHISELS
Straight (left) and cranked chisel (right). Use together with the mallet to remove tacks from frames. Use in the direction of the grain to prevent the wood from splintering.

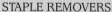

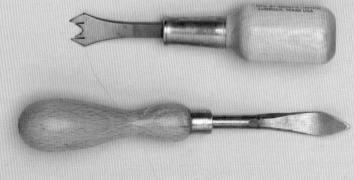

STAPLE REMOVERS
Berry staple remover (top) and standard staple remover (bottom). Push the end of the staple remover down and under the staple with the aid of a mallet. When firmly under the staple, push the handle down and ease the staple out. Use pincers for any broken pieces left in the frame.

PINCERS
Good for removing any broken ends of
staples or tacks. Grip the staple and work
the pincers with a rolling motion to remove.

WOODEN
MALLET
Use together with
a ripping chisel
to remove tacks
from frames.

GENERAL PROTECTION
Choose a heavy-duty apron that you don't mind getting dirty.
Eye and mouth protection is essential – dust from a chair whose
previous life is unknown can be pretty nasty.

Rebuilding tools

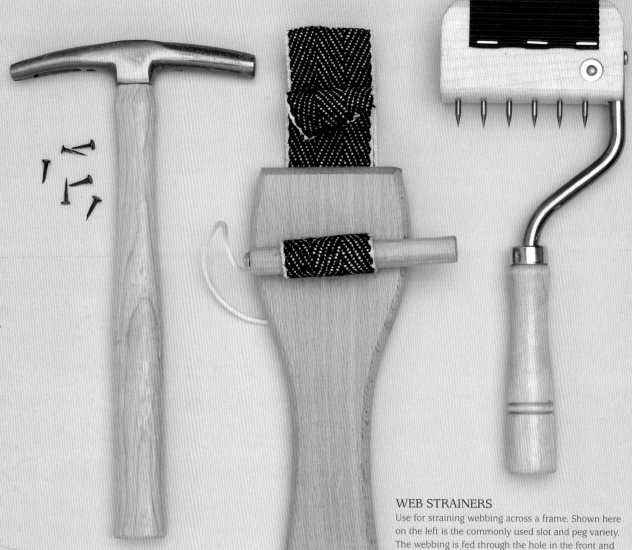

HAMMER

Use a specialist upholstery hammer for driving home tacks and decorative nails; the majority come with a magnetic end, useful for picking up and positioning tacks. The nylon-tipped variety protects the heads of the upholstery nails. If you can't find a nylon-tipped hammer, tape some polyester wadding to the end of your existing hammer. A capriole hammer has a much smaller tip on one end, which is good for working near show wood.

WEB STRAINERS

Use for straining webbing across a frame. Shown here on the left is the commonly used slot and peg variety. The webbing is fed through the hole in the front and secured with the peg in the back. The end is then anchored on the edge of the frame. Shown on the right is the gooseneck, which holds the webbing in its teeth. Pull the webbing very tight, but not so much that you hear the frame crack. Never pull webbing across a frame by hand – it will not be tight enough.

REGULATOR

Mostly used for the regulation of stuffing to keep it even and
lump free. The flat end is useful for flattening and shaping pleats.

SHARP BAYONET NEEDLE

Used for making top and blind stitching as well as stuffing ties. One end has an
eye for twine, the opposite end is sharp and flat for working through tough materials.

ROUNDED BUTTONING NEEDLE

More commonly used for buttoning. One end
has an eye, the other is smooth and rounded.

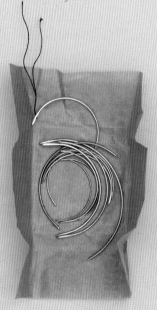

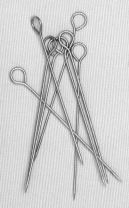

SPRING NEEDLE

Used to attach springs
to webbing and hessian.

PINS

Generally of a heavier weight
than standard pins used in soft
furnishings or dressmaking.

SKEWERS

Larger versions of upholstery pins.
They can hold fabric in place where
a tack or staple couldn't do the job,
for example holding a pleat in
position temporarily.

CURVED NEEDLES

Come in a variety of sizes. The
larger ones are good for bridle
ties. The smaller versions are
used for delicate slip stitching.

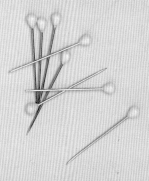

Measuring & cutting tools

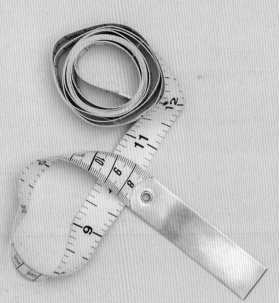

TAPE MEASURE
Use for measuring anything from fabric to frame sizes to upholstery nail spacing.

TAILOR'S CHALK
Use for marking out fabric cutting lines. Also for marking web or stitch spacing on frames.

STANLEY KNIFE
Useful for all kinds of jobs and essential for any toolkit.

FABRIC SHEARS
Shears are large, heavy scissors, ideal for cutting fabric. Do not use these for general cutting and make sure to keep them sharp.

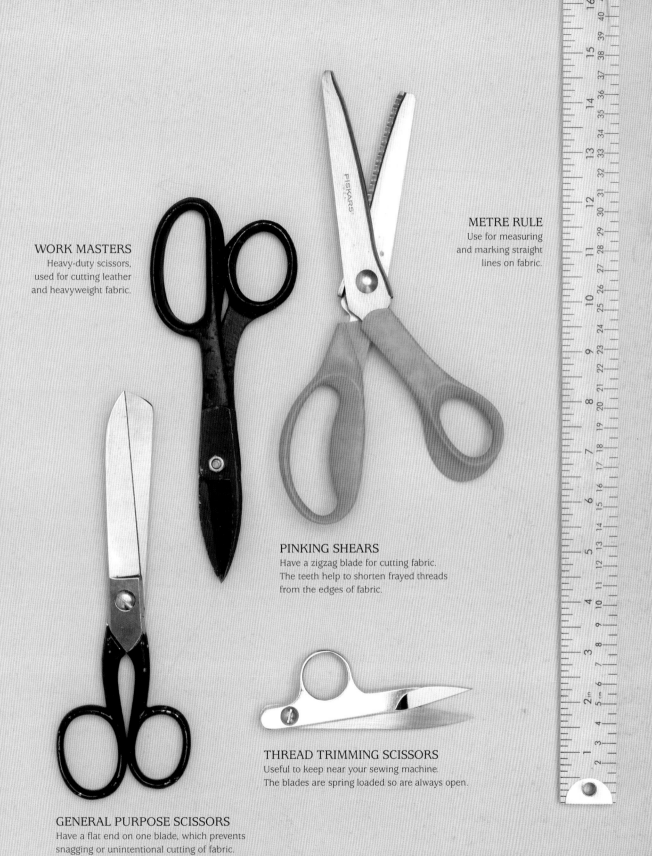

WORK MASTERS
Heavy-duty scissors, used for cutting leather and heavyweight fabric.

METRE RULE
Use for measuring and marking straight lines on fabric.

PINKING SHEARS
Have a zigzag blade for cutting fabric. The teeth help to shorten frayed threads from the edges of fabric.

THREAD TRIMMING SCISSORS
Useful to keep near your sewing machine. The blades are spring loaded so are always open.

GENERAL PURPOSE SCISSORS
Have a flat end on one blade, which prevents snagging or unintentional cutting of fabric.

Power & specialist tools

TACKS
Available as either 'improved' or 'fine', which refers to the thickness of the tack head. Come in a variety of sizes: 16mm (⅝in) improved, 13mm (½in) improved and fine, 10mm (⅜in) improved and fine and 6mm (¼in) fine.

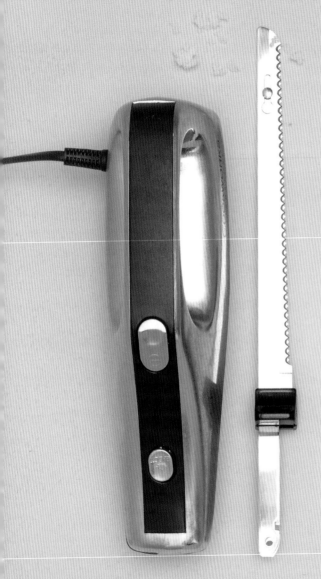

CARVING KNIFE
Used for cutting pieces of foam. Mark a straight line across the top of the foam and also down the sides. This will ensure a straight finish. Heavy-duty table top varieties are available, but cheap hand-held versions like the one above are fine for most home projects.

STAPLE GUN
An electric stapler is far more effective than a hand-held gun. The compressed air version shown above is more often seen in a professional upholstery workshop, but the electric version is perfectly adequate for home upholstery.

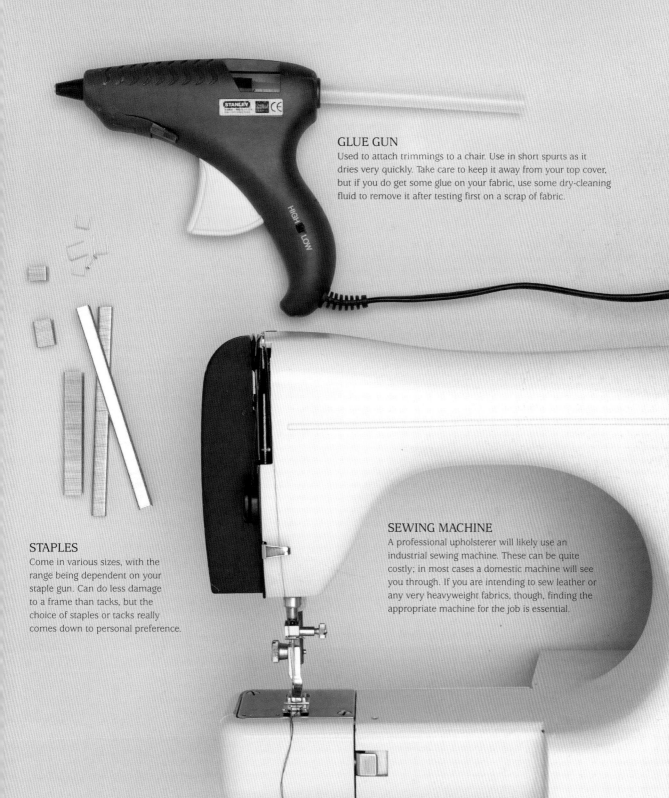

GLUE GUN

Used to attach trimmings to a chair. Use in short spurts as it dries very quickly. Take care to keep it away from your top cover, but if you do get some glue on your fabric, use some dry-cleaning fluid to remove it after testing first on a scrap of fabric.

STAPLES

Come in various sizes, with the range being dependent on your staple gun. Can do less damage to a frame than tacks, but the choice of staples or tacks really comes down to personal preference.

SEWING MACHINE

A professional upholsterer will likely use an industrial sewing machine. These can be quite costly; in most cases a domestic machine will see you through. If you are intending to sew leather or any very heavyweight fabrics, though, finding the appropriate machine for the job is essential.

Fillings

COIR
Fibre derived from the husk of a coconut.
It is quite coarse and is used for first stuffings.

WOOLLEN FELT
Made of a mix of woollen fibres, which give felt its multi-coloured, recycled look. The woven fibres make a strong wadding.

BLACK FIBRE
A vegetable fibre that has been treated and dyed to make it more durable than coir. Great for first stuffings and making firm edges.

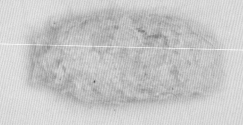

COTTON FELT
Sometimes known as linter felt. An incredibly soft and thick white cotton that comes in rolls held together with paper (which should be removed). Great for covering hair, coir or fibre as it prevents these materials from working through to the top cover.

ANIMAL HAIR
Soft and durable hair mainly taken from the tails and manes of horses. Cheaper alternatives are from cows and pigs. Used as a second stuffing in traditional upholstery.

SKIN WADDING
Soft cotton fibres covered in a skin-like material. Used before the top fabric, it prevents hairs from protruding through the top cover.

RUBBERISED HAIR
A mix of hair and rubber combined to give a uniform filling. Great for creating the shape of a piece in a matter of minutes – instant gratification! Make sure that the skin side is face up. Rubberised hair is hypoallergenic.

POLYESTER WADDING
Ideal for covering the foam in modern upholstery projects. It prevents friction between the foam and the fabric. Available in many thicknesses and is hypoallergenic.

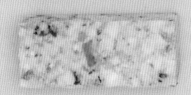

RECONSTITUTED FOAM
A mix of recycled foam pieces bonded together. Available in various grades. Check that it conforms to fire safety regulations in your country. Foam can be hypoallergenic, but check this with your supplier.

POLYURETHANE FOAM
The most commonly used filling in modern upholstery. Available in many grades or densities. It is usually sold in large sheets, but can be cut to size by your supplier. Check that it conforms to fire safety regulations in your country. Can be hypoallergenic, but check this with your supplier.

Linings

HESSIAN AND SCRIM

Coarse woven cloth made from jute, used for lining and support. Comes in various weights, each with their own uses. 7oz hessian (top left) is for use over webbings. 10oz hessian (middle) is medium weight and is used for lining backs and arms. Because of its weight, 12oz hessian (bottom left) is used for covering springs. Scrim (above) is more flexible than hessian and so gives a better shape, which is ideal for covering first layers of stuffing and for traditional stitched-edge work.

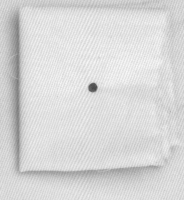

PLATFORM LININGS

A cotton lining slightly thicker than bottoming cloth and available in a few colours. Used for making the platform under a cushion or for making a fly.

BOTTOMING CLOTH

A professional finishing cloth for the bottoms of chairs. Similar in appearance to platform lining, but of lesser quality and strength.

CALICO

A woven cotton fabric used as a lining. Also used to take the strain of the final shape of the chair instead of the top fabric.

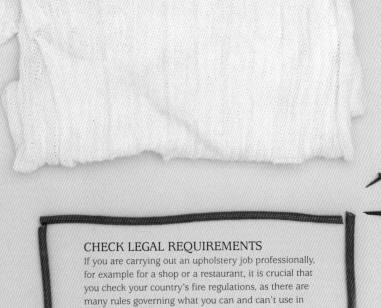

STOCKINETTE

A stretchy, stocking-like material, usually a polyester/synthetic mix. Stockinette should be wrapped around foam to prevent friction between the foam and the top cover in a similar way to polyester wadding.

CHECK LEGAL REQUIREMENTS

If you are carrying out an upholstery job professionally, for example for a shop or a restaurant, it is crucial that you check your country's fire regulations, as there are many rules governing what you can and can't use in a commercial setting.

Sundries

TWINES

Standard cord (left) used for sewing springs to webbing and hessian is 4-cord; it is also used for stitched-edge work. It is made from hemp, flax or jute. 3-cord is also available, but can only be used for very light stitch work; generally it's best to either use 4-cord or nylon twine. Nylon twine (right) has more longevity than natural twines, as it doesn't degrade over time. It's great for use in deep buttoning (tufting) and for stitched-edge work.

BACK TACKING CARD

Used to attach top covers to outside arms and backs. The card is placed under the top cover so that the attaching method is concealed. Alternatives are the metal ply grip or curve ease.

LAID CORD

Thick cord made from flax with little twist, therefore unlikely to stretch. Great for lashing springs into position.

PIPING CORD

Twisted cord made from cotton, which is the most commonly used piping cord in upholstery. Available as standard or pre-shrunk. The pre-shrunk type should be used when making up piped cushions that will likely be washed. Smooth cord is untwisted and covered in stockinette. Many synthetic cords are available, used mainly on modern furniture. Cord is available in different sizes – 3mm, 4mm, 5mm, or 6mm for example, or fine, medium, or heavy. Double-piping cord is available to buy, but you can also make up double piping using two single cords.

WEBBING

The supportive platform for springs, stuffing, top cover and the sitter. Lesser quality webbing is used in arms and backs and for drop-in seats. Elastic webbings are made of woven rubber and synthetic yarns. These are commonly used on modern chairs and have clips for fixing to frames.

SLIPPING THREAD

Made from flax and treated with wax during production. Comes in a variety of colours. Use for hand sewing during the finishing process.

SPRAY ADHESIVE

Essential for securing foam pads in position. Other uses include bonding rubberised hair and cut edges of polyester together. Use with a plastic dust sheet to protect other items from the glue.

Fixings

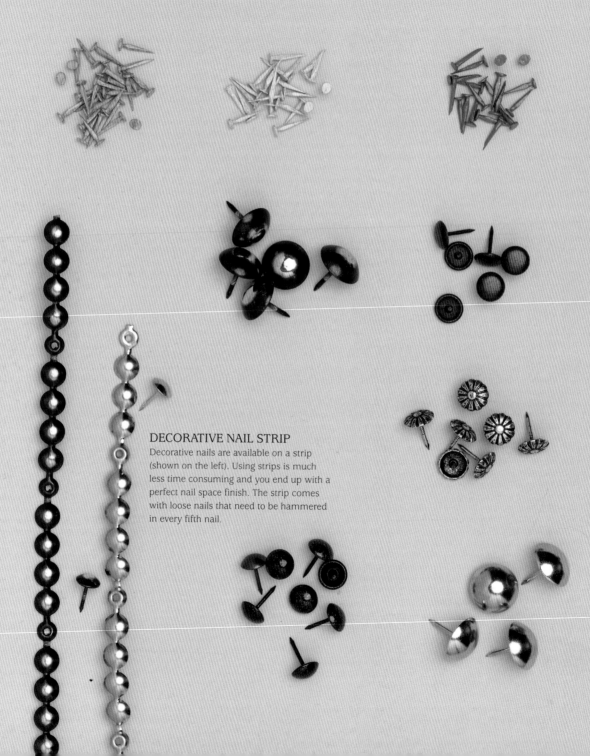

DECORATIVE NAIL STRIP

Decorative nails are available on a strip (shown on the left). Using strips is much less time consuming and you end up with a perfect nail space finish. The strip comes with loose nails that need to be hammered in every fifth nail.

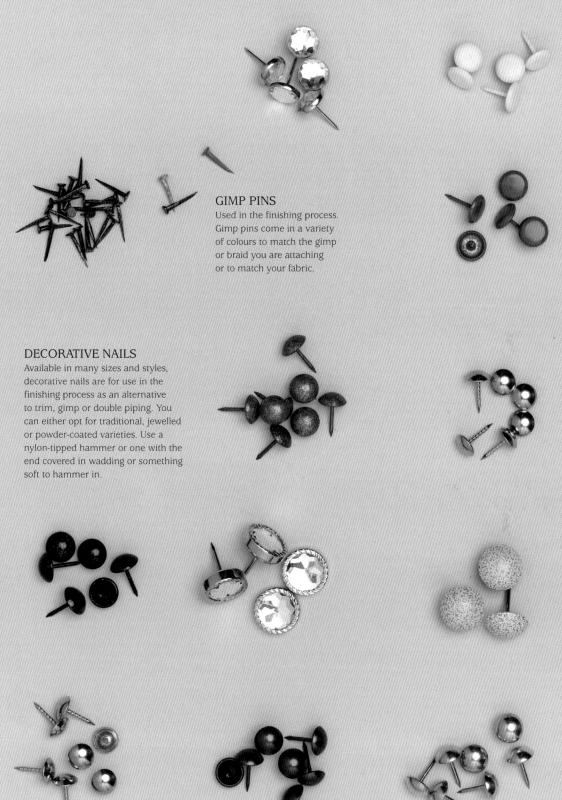

GIMP PINS

Used in the finishing process. Gimp pins come in a variety of colours to match the gimp or braid you are attaching or to match your fabric.

DECORATIVE NAILS

Available in many sizes and styles, decorative nails are for use in the finishing process as an alternative to trim, gimp or double piping. You can either opt for traditional, jewelled or powder-coated varieties. Use a nylon-tipped hammer or one with the end covered in wadding or something soft to hammer in.

Trimmings

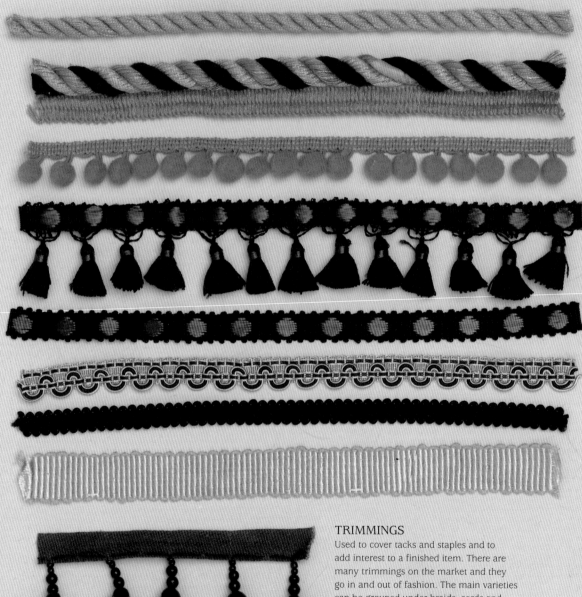

TRIMMINGS

Used to cover tacks and staples and to add interest to a finished item. There are many trimmings on the market and they go in and out of fashion. The main varieties can be grouped under braids, cords and fringes. Attached with a combination of hot glue and coloured gimp pins.

BUTTON MAKER

A professional button maker is an expensive piece of equipment, but can be very useful. There are also a few inexpensive substitutes on the market for making your own buttons, or a local upholsterer will be able to make up buttons for you.

Frame stripping

BICARBONATE OF SODA

Once you've used paint stripper on your frame, you'll need to remove the residue and neutralise. Mix bicarbonate of soda with lukewarm water and wipe onto the frame with a plastic scourer. Rinse with water.

PAINT STRIPPER

All paint strippers follow a similar process: thickly dab the solution onto the item, wait a while, then scrape off. Follow the instructions on the tin.

WIRE WOOL

Thicker grades – 2, 3 and 4 – are used for stripping; finer grades – 0, 00 and 000 – are used for dulling a finish; grade 0000 is for cleaning. Do not rip wire wool with your hands, use an old pair of scissors.

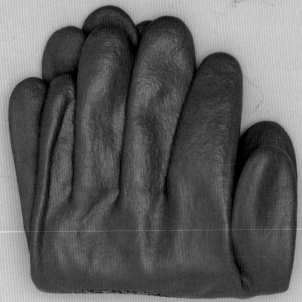

PAINT SCRAPER

Used to remove the majority of the paint stripper from the frame. Follow with wire wool for deeper paint and varnish removal.

GLOVES AND FACEMASK

Many of the substances used in the stripping process are harmful, so it is essential to have some heavy-duty gloves and a facemask in your toolkit.

VINEGAR AND WATER

Use with a soft cloth to clean the surface. Mix together and dispense from a spray bottle. Do not use to clean a waxed surface.

OXALIC ACID

A bleach used to remove marks in the wood. Supplied as crystals that must be dissolved in water and applied to a surface with a brush. Follow the manufacturer's instructions and wear protective clothing. After application, the surface must be neutralised with water.

METHYLATED SPIRIT AND VINEGAR

You can buy ready-made wood revivers or you can make your own: mix one part methylated spirit and one part vinegar in a glass jar. Apply with a soft cloth. Do not use on a French polished surface. Will also remove wax.

WHITE SPIRIT AND RAW LINSEED OIL

Use together with the finest grade wire wool to clean varnished wood. Clean off with a scrap of calico. Do not use to clean bare timber as the oil will soak into the wood and make it darker. Will also remove wax from wood. Mix together 5 per cent oil and 95 per cent white spirit in a glass jar.

Frame care & repair

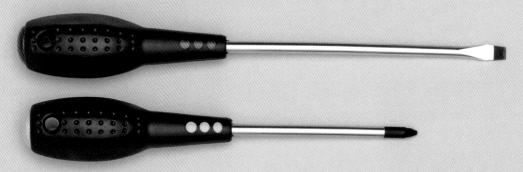

SCREWDRIVERS

The most common types are 'flat-head' for use with slotted screws, and 'Phillips' for use with crosshead screws.

DRILL

Used for making holes for screws and dowels. Various drill bit sizes are available and it's a good idea to invest in a countersink attachment. Can also be used with a screwdriver attachment to drive screws.

SCREWS AND DOWELS

Screws (shown on the left) are used in conjunction with PVA or wood glue to fix and hold frames together. Dowel joints (shown on the right) are often used in the repair of chair frames. For added strength, use two or three dowels for every joint. A hole is drilled between two parts of a frame that are clamped together. The dowel is then glued and hammered into the hole and left to dry while still clamped.

PVA AND SAWDUST

Mix PVA glue and very fine sawdust to make a strong filler for frames. This paste can be scraped into tack holes with a spatula. You may need to lightly sand the area once dried to prevent damage to any upholstery materials. Tinted wood filler is suitable for filling holes on show wood.

WOODWORM TREATMENTS

Research the various treatments available, as many are pretty nasty. There are some that only target the furniture beetle and will not harm any other animal. Always wear protective clothing and follow the instructions on the tin.

SANDPAPER

A sheet coated with abrasive. Comes in various grit sizes, with 80-grit being very coarse and 240-grit being very fine. You must sand the frame before upholstering – any sharp pieces of wood could rip your fabric. The sandpaper pictured above is wrapped around a cork block for sanding flat surfaces.

Frame care & repair

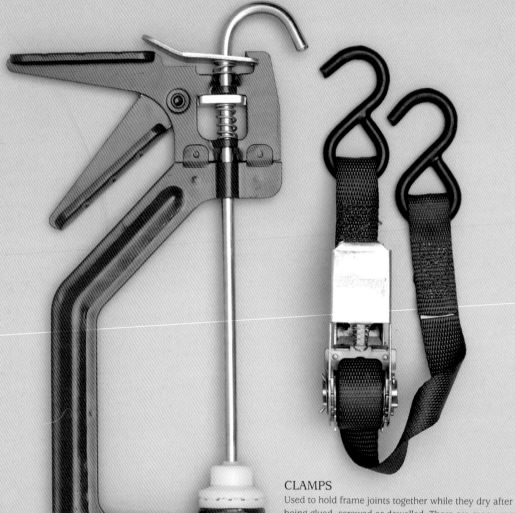

CLAMPS

Used to hold frame joints together while they dry after being glued, screwed or dowelled. There are many versions available. The ratchet strap clamp shown above is good for wrapping around whole frames. The clamp on the left is handy for holding frames to the bench while ripping down.

RASP

The edge of a frame in traditional upholstery needs to have a bevelled edge to tack onto. Use the rasp to either make or perfect this edge. The rasp can leave a coarse finish, so smooth off with some sandpaper.

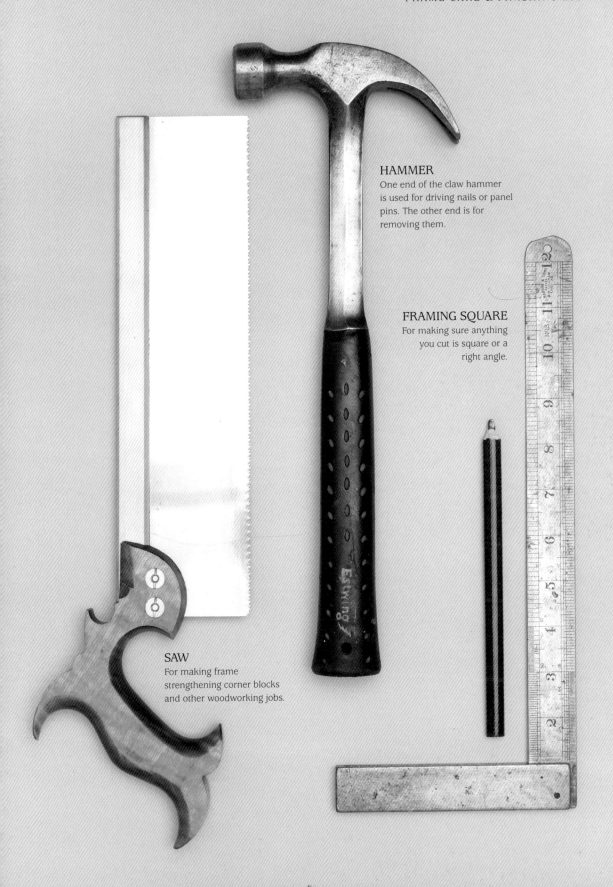

HAMMER
One end of the claw hammer is used for driving nails or panel pins. The other end is for removing them.

FRAMING SQUARE
For making sure anything you cut is square or a right angle.

SAW
For making frame strengthening corner blocks and other woodworking jobs.

Frame care & repair

SHELLAC SANDING SEALER
Used on untreated wood as a base
for coating with shellac or wax.

WAX
Leaves a natural finished look, which improves over
time with constant handling deepening the patina.
There are many different colours of wax on the market.

WAX STICKS
Available in many wood colours.
Good for filling small holes and
scratches in show wood.

STAINS
Many different stains are available,
each with their own characteristics
in terms of drying time and colour
range. Test out the colour on a
hidden area before committing
to your frame.

TACK CLOTH
Cloth that is tacky to the touch. Great for
removing dust and dirt from surfaces in
preparation for applying your next finish.

PAINTS

Primer makes for better paint adhesion and protects
the wood. This should be followed by a layer of undercoat,
but there are paints that combine the two stages. Topcoats
come in a variety of finishes, from eggshell to high gloss.
Use a brush or roller to apply, or for an even smoother
finish, buy your paint in a spray can.

ROLLERS AND BRUSHES

Smaller rollers are ideal for painting
wood. These come with synthetic or
mohair sleeves and are great for giving
an even, smooth finish.

MASKING TAPE

Useful for covering areas that need
to be protected. It's not particularly
sticky, so is easy to remove once the
work is complete.

SECTION 2

Working With Fabrics

Cloudbirds fabric by Skinny laMinx.

Fabric characteristics

All fabrics are made from either natural or synthetic fibres or, more often than not, a combination of both. Common natural fibres include cotton, wool and silk; synthetics include polyester, acrylic and vinyl. Blends of both families were developed either to imitate or to improve on a specific natural fibre. A blend of a natural fibre with nylon, for example, increases its strength and helps guard against stains. The addition of polyester adds wrinkle resistance and reduces the chances of fading.

The chart on the following pages gives an overview of some common upholstery fabrics, their pros and cons and a few usage tips.

			MOST SUITED TO	PROS	CONS
ECO FABRIC	CORK		• Good for high-traffic areas, such as sofas	• Sustainable, renewable and environmentally friendly • Hard-wearing • Easy to clean • Waterproof and stain resistant • Soft to the touch • Dust, dirt and grease repellent	• Can be bulky; not suitable for a delicate chair
	HEMP		• All types of furniture	• Sustainable • Fast growing without the use of chemicals • Inherently fire retardant • Comes in over 30 colours • Highly durable	• None
	NETTLE		• All types of furniture	• Sustainable • Soft • Strong fibres • Naturally fire retardant • Highly durable	• None

DURABILITY	TIPS FOR WORKING WITH	CLEANING & CARE	PET RESISTANCE
• Highly durable	• Has elastic properties and can be stretched or shaped in any direction • Much like leather	• Can be washed using just a damp cloth and a very light detergent • Cork cushion covers can be machine washed	• Because of cork's anti-grease and dirt-resistant properties, it's incredibly pet friendly
• Highly durable	• Soft and malleable • Has good give, making it easy to work with	• Dry-clean any loose covers • Never over-wet wool/hemp blend; it acts in the same way as wool, so will shrink	• Hemp isn't deep-pile so any dust or dried dirt can be brushed off • Vacuum regularly
• Highly durable	• A wool/nettle blend is easy to work with, as it has good give and can be easily manipulated	• Do not over-wet a wool/nettle blend as it will shrink	• Nettle isn't deep-pile so any dust or dried dirt can be brushed off • Vacuum regularly

		MOST SUITED TO	PROS	CONS
COTTON	CHINTZ	• Screens • Headboards • Slipcovers	• Colour has more depth than when printed on plain cotton • Practical; dust won't settle easily • Highly hypoallergenic	• Patterns will fade over time • The surface may crack (especially if overglazed) • Creases are impossible to remove, so always keep on the roll, not folded
	COTTON	• All types of furniture • Slipcovers and bottom cloth	• Lightweight and easy to work with • Inexpensive • Durable • Holds colour well • Good resistance to pilling • Generally hypoallergenic	• Can ravel with regular use • May shrink – if you wash your slipcovers, let them dry naturally • Prone to wrinkling • Stains easily • May stretch over time
	COTTON DUCK	• Outdoor furniture	• Durable • Dyes well • Easy to work with • Good resistance to pilling • Good for outdoor use • Highly hypoallergenic	• Not suitable for delicate pieces of furniture where there are many pleats and corners • Can be too thick for some uses • Not very comfortable to the touch • Stains easily
	OILCLOTH	• Kitchen tables • Simple patio chairs • Stools • Cushions	• Waterproof • Does not fray	• Quite stiff if using as upholstery • Difficult to pleat • Difficult to sew • Non-biodegradable • The PVC covering can be harmful for children; in the USA, oilcloth is prohibited for use in baby and children's products
	TICKING	• Light upholstery in low-traffic areas • Cushions	• Lightweight and easy to work with • Inexpensive • Good resistance to pilling • Generally hypoallergenic	• Not suitable for heavy-traffic areas • Stains easily

DURABILITY	TIPS FOR WORKING WITH	CLEANING & CARE	PET RESISTANCE
• Fairly durable	• Easy to sew • Can wrinkle, so keep taut when upholstering • Keep rolled before use, not folded	• Gently wipe clean – the polished surface can be easily damaged • Vacuum on a low setting • If used as a slipcover, it can be dry-cleaned • Iron on a low setting and press on the reverse	• Pet hairs dust off easily
• Highly durable	• Has good give and is an easy textile to work with • Creases easily, so always keep on the roll when not in use	• Apply a stain-resistant finish (test on a small area first) • Remove stains with warm water and a little neutral soap • Rinse with clean water • Do not rub too hard as this will leave marks	• Pet hair can be dusted or vacuumed off • Can stain easily if not protected with a stain guard
• Highly durable	• Use pre-shrunk if making slipcovers • Keep on the roll rather than folded	• Apply a stain-resistant finish (test on a small area first) • Vacuum regularly • Can be machine washed	• Pet hair can be dusted or vacuumed off • Can stain easily if not protected with a stain guard
• Highly durable	• To stop the oilcloth from sticking while sewing, place another piece of oilcloth face down on the machine just in front of the needle. Use a Teflon foot on the machine. Alternatively, place a piece of tissue paper on the top and bottom of the fabric being sewn. Carefully remove once sewn	• Simply wipe clean with soapy water and a sponge	• Sharp claws can puncture the oilcloth
• Moderately durable	• Has good give and is easy to work with • Creases easily, so always keep on the roll when not in use	• Apply a stain-resistant finish (test on a small area first) • Remove stains with warm water and a little neutral soap • Rinse with clean water • Do not rub too hard as this will leave marks	• Pet hair can be dusted or vacuumed off • Can stain easily if not protected with a stain guard

		MOST SUITED TO	PROS	CONS
WOOL	FELT	• Looks great on anything, with its seamless, flat appearance	• Moisture resistant • Warm • Recyclable • Non-directional and doesn't ravel • Great colourways available	• Depending on the thickness of the felt, you may find it difficult to sew using a domestic machine
	OLEFIN	• Outdoor furniture	• Lightweight • Fade resistant • Mould and mildew resistant • Holds vibrant colours well • Relatively environmentally friendly due to the few by-products produced during manufacturing • Tough and hard-wearing • Economical • Hypoallergenic	• Flammable – will melt if exposed to high heat • Attracts oil stains • Pills easily • Highly static
	TARTAN	• Outdoor furniture	• Durable • Dyes well • Easy to work with • Good resistance to pilling • Highly hypoallergenic	• Not suitable for delicate pieces of furniture where there are many pleats and corners • Can be too thick for some uses • Not very comfortable to the touch • Stains easily
	TWEED	• Can be used on all types of furniture • Hard-wearing, so can be used in high-traffic areas	• Unlikely to fade • Doesn't crease or wrinkle • Warm in winter, cool in summer • Hard-wearing • Great colourways • Raw wool is hypoallergenic, but check with your supplier	• Can be a little coarse
	WOOL	• Highly resilient and can withstand high traffic • Use on any item of furniture • Widely used on public seating	• Water repellent • Hard-wearing • Warm in winter, cool in summer • Natural fire resistance • Anti-static • Biodegradable • Fantastic range of colours • Soft to the touch • Raw wool is hypoallergenic, but check with your supplier	• None

DURABILITY	TIPS FOR WORKING WITH	CLEANING & CARE	PET RESISTANCE
• Highly durable	• If you have something quite shapely to upholster, choose the thinner variety • Use a knife for precise cutting	• Do not put in the washing machine or dryer • Spot clean with warm soapy water • Do not saturate	• Has great resistance to dirt, so is fine around animals
• Highly durable	• Can be slightly stiff, but is easy to work with	• Do not dry-clean • Water-based stains can easily be wiped off • Oil-based stains can sometimes be removed with lukewarm water and detergent; check with the supplier or on an out-of-sight area first	• Good for use around pets because of its strength and stain-resistant qualities
• Highly durable	• Use pre-shrunk if making slipcovers • Keep on the roll rather than folded	• Apply a stain-resistant finish • Vacuum regularly • Can be machine washed	• Pet hair can be dusted or vacuumed off • Can stain easily if not protected with a stain guard
• Highly durable	• Has good give, so can be shaped and pulled	• Check any labels or with the supplier before cleaning • Will likely need to be dry-cleaned • Clean fixed upholstery regularly with a vacuum cleaner • Stains can be removed with a damp towel, working in a circular motion • Do not saturate	• Durable and hard-wearing; a good choice for a household with pets
• Highly durable	• Lovely to use • Very soft and malleable • Has good give	• Weekly light vacuuming will remove dust and dirt	• Fine to use around pets, as it resists stains and dirt and is incredibly hard-wearing

		MOST SUITED TO	PROS	CONS
DEEP PILE	CHENILLE	• Large pieces of furniture that can take the thickness of the fabric	• Soft to the touch • Durable	• Can fray easily • The pile can crush • If made from silk, it can trigger allergic reactions
	CORDUROY	• Quite durable, so can go on any piece of furniture, but often looks better on larger pieces rather than anything delicate and fine	• Soft to the touch • Durable • Hypoallergenic	• None
	MOQUETTE	• Bus and train seating	• Incredibly hard-wearing • Fade resistant • Comfortable • Warm in the winter and cool in the summer • Stain resistant • Highly hypoallergenic	• Can feel too 'utilitarian'
	VELVET	• Low-traffic areas • Show pieces • Headboards	• Luxurious to look at • Soft to the touch	• Difficult to clean • Creases and flattens easily • Wears quickly • Vulnerable to moths • Can be expensive, depending on the blend
SILK	SILK	• Not suited to high-traffic areas; better for a show piece or bedroom chair • Good for headboards	• Crease resistant • Luxurious look and feel	• Very delicate • Not very hard-wearing • Difficult to clean • Will rot in direct sunlight • Highly flammable • Has been known to trigger asthma and allergic rhinitis

DURABILITY	TIPS FOR WORKING WITH	CLEANING & CARE	PET RESISTANCE
• Durable	• Use fray check on any exposed cuts	• Vacuum regularly on a low setting. Don't use water or cleaning products on tougher stains – seek advice from your supplier first. If they suggest an upholstery shampoo, make sure not to over-wet. Blot any excess moisture with a clean and dry cloth. Test any products on an out-of-sight area first	• Not suited for pets
• Durable	• Can be quite thick, so take care when upholstering a chair with many pleats	• Always keep on the roll to protect from damage • Gentle, occasional vacuuming • If using a brush, always use in one direction to preserve the nap. Brushing in the wrong direction will cause the fabric to look rough. Keep on the roll and do not fold before use	• Can withstand a small amount of animal abuse
• Highly durable	• A very forgiving fabric; if it gets damaged, it can be easily fixed without leaving too many scars	• Vacuum occasionally • Rarely stains	• Good for pets as there is very little wear
• Not very durable	• Cut and position the fabric with the pile running down the chair • If it's a complicated chair with many cuts and pleats, try to sort any potential problems with the calico layer to avoid damaging the fabric • Keep on a roll when not in use; do not fold	• Steam-clean large pieces of furniture • Apply stain guard (test a small piece of fabric first) • Work fabric shampoo in the direction of the pile or nap and use a soft brush • Vacuum regularly • Brush the pile with a clean, damp cloth to release creases	• Keep pets and children away from velvet; any hair or dirt will work its way into the pile and be difficult to remove
• Quite durable	• Has a surprising amount of give, making it quite easy to work with	• Vacuum to remove loose dirt • Clean with a soft cloth and a mixture of cold water and a mild laundry detergent • Do not over-wet as you could be left with water marks • Any loose covers may be dry-cleaned, but check with supplier first	• Keep pets well away from silk

PATTERNED AND EMBELLISHED

		MOST SUITED TO	PROS	CONS
CREWEL		• Curtains and show pieces	• Luxurious	• Tricky to clean
DAMASK		• Because of its luxurious appearance, it's best suited to show pieces or furniture that are unlikely to come into contact with children and animals	• Luxurious and elegant looking • Easy to work with • Reversible	• If made from silk, it can trigger allergic reactions
BROCADE		• Light upholstery and curtains • Looks good on period furniture	• Luxurious looking	• Tricky to clean • Can snag and fray easily • Can be a bit bulky • Silk has been known to trigger asthma and allergic rhinitis
MATELASSE		• Often used for bedspreads, but also suitable for large pieces of furniture, slipcovers and cushions	• Interesting look and feel • Cotton based, so is hypoallergenic • Soft	• Can be quite bulky to work with • Can tear easily
TAPESTRY		• Anything from large pieces of furniture to footstools and wall hangings	• Hard-wearing	• Can be heavy, thick and bulky

DURABILITY	TIPS FOR WORKING WITH	CLEANING & CARE	PET RESISTANCE
• Durable	• The embroidery can be quite thick, so think about this when planning on deep buttoning or covering a piece of furniture requiring many pleats. Can be difficult to manoeuvre	• Doesn't attract dust so can be just brushed or lightly vacuumed occasionally, but if the embroidery takes up most of the fabric, then cleaning is more of an issue. Dirt can become lodged in the embroidery. Creases easily, so keep on the roll before using	• Keep pets away
• Durable	• Very easy to work with. Looks great deep buttoned	• Use a soft brush or a vacuum cleaner on a low setting to remove any loose dirt. You will probably need to use a dry-cleaning solution for heavy stains. Refer to the supplier's instructions and test on an out-of-sight area. Keep out of direct sunlight	• Keep pets away from silk damask
• Durable	• Frays easily, use fray check where necessary. Can be quite bulky, so consider this when thinking about deep buttoning or using on a chair with many pleats	• Clean with a soft cloth and a mixture of cold water and a mild laundry detergent. Do not over-wet as you could be left with water marks. Test a small area first. For spot cleaning, use a dry-cleaning solution. Test on scrap or out-of-sight pieces of fabric first. Keep away from direct sunlight	• Keep pets away
• Durable	• Quite heavyweight and also bulky. Not suitable for delicate pieces of furniture needing a lot of pleating	• If being used as a slipcover or cushion, take care when washing. Prone to shrinking. Vacuum regularly on a low setting	• Fairly safe to use in a pet area
• Highly durable	• Tapestry can sometimes be quite bulky, so use on furniture with simple lines and minimal pleating	• Remove any dust or dirt with a vacuum cleaner on a low setting. Test some upholstery shampoo on an out-of-sight area for spot cleaning. Try not to over-wet the fabric. Expensive or antique tapestries should be professionally cleaned	• Keep pets away from tapestry

			MOST SUITED TO	PROS	CONS
ANIMAL	HORSEHAIR		• Show piece dining room chairs, simple seating, and decorative panels	• Luxurious • Easy to clean • Incredibly tough, so wear-resisting	• Can be a little stiff
	LEATHER		• Pieces that will receive heavy wear and need to last a long time	• Tough • Available in many colours and finishes • Resistant to staining • Good for high-traffic areas • Improves with age	• May be uncomfortable to sit on with bare legs • Might not appeal to people concerned about animal welfare • The hide may be covered with scars and insect bites; a better-quality hide will have less, but will cost more • You will need an industrial sewing machine to sew it
	MICROFIBRE		• High-traffic areas	• Wrinkle free • Doesn't pill • Stain resistant • Soft to the touch	• Can be very static • The manufacturing process is not very eco-friendly • Flammable
	VINYL		• Public seating, such as bars, hotels and car interiors. Also suitable for use in hospitals and care homes	• Relatively inexpensive • Durable • Good stretch, making it easy to work with • Waterproof, so high resistance to dirt and mildew • The PVC covering can be harmful for children; in the USA, oilcloth is prohibited for use in baby and children's products	• Can feel a little 'institutional'
PLANT	LINEN		• Slipcovers • Cushion covers • Headboards	• Strong fibre • Very cool to the touch • Antistatic • Hypoallergenic	• Not very flexible • Susceptible to creasing

DURABILITY	TIPS FOR WORKING WITH	CLEANING & CARE	PET RESISTANCE
• Highly durable	• Quite stiff, so not that easily manoeuvrable around corners or into pleats	• Brush or vacuum the fabric regularly. Wipe any spillages with a damp cloth and again with a dry cloth. Do not over-wet or leave any liquids on the fabric. Seek specialist cleaning advice for heavier stains	• The hair is highly durable, but it's advisable to keep pets away from such a special fabric
• Highly durable	• Unlike fabric, there is no wrong direction to pull or cut; it simply eases in any direction you move it • You can shrink leather with heat, which can help if you're trying to loosen a pleat	• Wipe with a soap-dampened cloth • Avoid positioning near a heat source • Remove any spills immediately with a dry cloth • Don't leave hot coffee cups on the arms; they will stain	• Pet hair can be easily removed from leather, but it can be marked by pets' claws. There are products on the market that can repair scratches and can even ward off cats! Test on an out-of-sight area first
• Highly durable	• A very flexible fabric. It has give in all directions, making it very easy to manipulate	• Animal hair or dirt doesn't embed in the weave, so simply vacuum to clean. You can also clean with a slightly damp cloth	• Can stand up to moderate pet abuse
• Good quality vinyls are highly durable	• Has good give, making it easy to work with	• Simply wipe off any dirt with a sponge and some soapy water. Do not use any wax polishes or solvents to clean; check cleaning instructions with the supplier or manufacturer first	• A good fabric to use in a pet loving household
• Highly durable	• Creases easily so keep on the roll when not in use • Has little give so can be difficult to manoeuvre	• Because of its anti-static qualities, linen doesn't attract dust • Simply brush the upholstery or gently vacuum it • If washing cushion covers, make sure the linen has been pre-shrunk	• Highly durable; will stand up well to general wear and tear

general considerations

It is inevitable that upholstery will change in appearance over its lifetime, but there are steps you can take to minimise this that don't include making arm protectors or covering the finished piece in plastic!

STORING

Any fabric you are keeping to use at a later date needs to be stored carefully. Rolling fabric rather than folding it and storing it flat will minimise creasing. Make sure your storage area is dry and check regularly for moths.

CHOOSING FABRIC

Think about the end use of the piece. Will it be in an area with children and pets? Or will it be more of a show piece/clothes horse in the bedroom? Refer to the information on pages 38–49 for advice on different types of fabric.

Chairs upholstered in Points fabric by Lisa Barrett for Tango & James.

Leaves fabrics by Skinny laMinx.

FABRIC QUALITY

When you buy fabric, it should be clearly labelled with information on the size and pattern repeat and any testing results. You'll find a reduced version of these results on the product label. They include:

- Rub test, or 'Martindale'
- Colour fade test
- Flammability

If you are buying fabric for use in your home and you love it, test results are mostly irrelevant. If you're upholstering a piece professionally, however, this information is really important. The last thing you want is for a chair to go up in smoke at the sound of a match being struck.

CLEANING

All fabrics have their own particular needs when it comes to cleaning, but vacuuming regularly or removing any dust with a soft brush are useful for all fabrics.

STAIN REMOVAL

Stain removal will depend on the fabric in question, but it's generally not good to soak the stain. Use a slightly damp cloth to remove any spills. Work towards the centre of the spill and don't rub too hard.

FADING

Keep furniture out of direct sunlight. Direct heat and strong sunlight can weaken the fibres; silks are particularly prone to fading. Most fabric deteriorates in bright sunlight, but the pattern on printed textiles will suffer quicker than, say, with a woven pattern. Also be aware that washing is likely to change the shade of a coloured fabric.

SHRINKAGE

If you're making loose covers or cushions that you intend to wash, make sure the fabric is pre-shrunk or wash it yourself. The same applies to piping. If you iron it while damp, you can stretch the fabric slightly. Check the manufacturer's instructions or test on an out-of-sight area.

MAINTENANCE

Plumping up cushions keeps upholstery looking fresh, and rotating them can also prolong their life, as it spreads the area of wear.

Fabric repairs

If your furniture lives with children, pets or the inherently clumsy, then it's likely to become damaged. However, a small tear or a popped button doesn't really call for a total upholstery overhaul.

Ripped fabric

YOU WILL NEED
- Good-quality thread in a matching colour. Slipping thread is ideal
- A small curved needle
- Fray check

1 Cover the frayed ends of the fabric with fray check.

2 Fold under the frayed edges, bring together and pin. Start with a slip knot and slip stitch the area together (see pages 110 and 114). Loose ends of thread can be lost in the upholstery by pulling the needle and thread back through the fabric.

Patching holes

YOU WILL NEED
- Fusible webbing
- Fabric piece
- Fray check

If the fabric is no longer on the market, check if there's some spare on the chair itself. This may be on the underside, although it may be a little brighter than the fabric you are patching. Follow these steps, but check any instructions that come with the webbing. If you intend to use heavyweight webbing, be sure to test first. Heavyweights can have a habit of seeping through some fabric.

1 Cut a piece of fabric just larger than your hole and slide under.

2 Cover the top fabric ends with some fray check and fold under. Cut some strips of fusible webbing and slide under the top fabric positioning close to the opening. Pin the sides in as closely to each other as possible.

3 Press with a warm iron on one side at a time.

Replacing buttons

YOU WILL NEED
- Nylon thread
- Button
- Auto-release button needle

It can be frustrating to have a button pop on you. Even more so if it means taking the back off the chair to repair it. Thankfully there are tools to help you re-button without the pain of re-upholstery.

1 If you don't have the original button, cut some spare fabric from under the frame. Cover a button using a buttonmaking kit or get one made by an upholsterer.

2 Thread the clasp on the auto-buttoner with some nylon twine. Insert the clasp into the end of the tool.

3 Push the needle through the fabric and into the stuffing. Take care at this point not to push the needle too far. Release the clasp by pressing in the plunger, then remove.

4 Thread the end of the twine through the button and make a slip knot. Tighten so that the button sits at the same depth as the other buttons. Tie a knot just at the end of the button to secure. Cut any exposed ends.

Ripped fabric 1

Patching holes 2

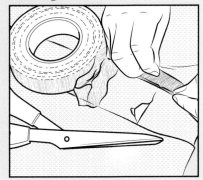

Replacing buttons 2

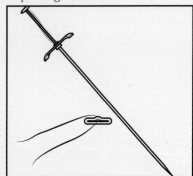

Ripped fabric 2

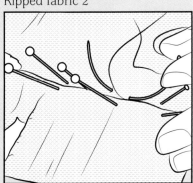

Patching holes 3

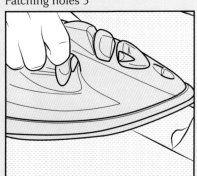

Replacing buttons 3

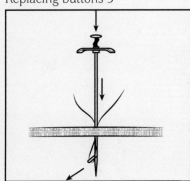

Patching holes 1

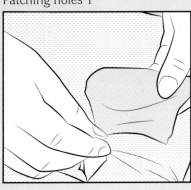

Replacing buttons 1

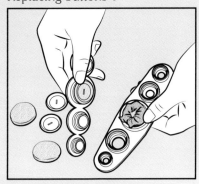

Replacing buttons 4

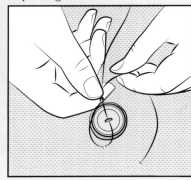

Fabric decisions

If you care enough about a piece of furniture to put in the time and effort to re-upholster it, you should put an equal amount of effort and imagination into choosing the right fabric. Visit small design exhibitions and student shows; look online and in charity shops. Don't be put off by high-end shops, either; try to get an overview of what's out there. There are of course magazines and a myriad of design blogs too, but rarely do these give you an idea of the feel and quality of the fabric itself.

Wild Flowers fabric by Skinny laMinx.

NARROWING DOWN THE CHOICE

Something new and 'must-have' is created every minute in the fabric world, so you need to be selective. First, consider the style and age of the chair, then research and collect swatches of pattern, texture and colour. Think about where the finished piece will live and what sort of use it will get, and the conditions it will need to withstand in its new home.

Sofa upholstered in Wild Flowers fabric by Skinny laMinx.

Style & age

The first part of the decision process might be to research the history of the chair you're upholstering. As you work, you'll uncover layers or pieces of fabric that are firmly locked in their time. And then there's the frame – this can have its own fascinating story to tell. It may be helpful to know the original covering and where or how the chair was used. Try to be sympathetic to its heritage, but not governed by it. For example, think twice before covering an original Louis chair in harsh geometrics or a deckchair in tapestry. The fabric needs to be as weighty as the frame you're covering; not in physical weight, but more in terms of quality and style.

In terms of the chair in a room as a whole, you might decide to mix and match styles. One idea is to unite all the furniture in a room using a common element – like a pattern, for example – so that it looks more considered and less charity shop. Taste, of course, is very subjective. You may want your home to pay homage to the 1950s, for instance. But remember that having too much of one style can feel like being stuck in a time warp – and how unimaginative would that be?

©GUBI. Bonaparte sofa by Gubi Olsen, Cobra table lamp by Greta M. Grossman and Kangourou side table by Mathieu Matégot.

Colour

Probably one of the most important decisions you'll make is regarding the colour. Colour can remind you of your grandma's avocado bathroom suite, of a great holiday or make you feel cold or even hungry. But more often than not, the use of colour comes down to fashion. I guess that's why you always encounter the 'neutral base, pop of colour' cliché. An easy seasonal colour change can be made with a new cushion or throw. However, try to avoid being a slave to fashion. There tend to be colours we are just naturally drawn to; if they work for you, great. But don't be scared to look outside of your comfort zone.

Colour wheel. Photo by Ryann Ford.

It's hard to talk about colour without mentioning the colour wheel. Understanding how the wheel works will save you so much time when choosing colours. The colour wheel starts with the primaries. Blue, red and yellow – every other colour is a mixture of these three. The secondary colours sit between the primaries and are the colours made when the primaries are combined. Tertiary colours are combinations of a primary and a secondary colour.

Chair and ottoman in Fanpods fabric by Lisa Barrett for Tango & James.

Detail of a footstool upholstered by Lucy Davidson.

1955 Fler SC55 armchair upholstered by Flourish and Blume.

Colours that sit opposite each other on the colour wheel are complementary. Blue and orange, say, or yellow and purple. Rather than bringing these colours together in blocks, try using one as the dominant colour and the other as a highlight. A blue chair with some orange piping, perhaps. Colours that sit next to each other on the wheel and are of the same hue are referred to as analogous. Yellow, yellow-green and green for example. These colours work well together because they are harmonious. Try adding a bit of contrast to keep such a scheme from looking flat.

The colour wheel can also be divided into cold and warm colours. Tone refers to how light or how dark a colour is. A colour with white added to it is called a tint, and a colour with black added to it is a shade. Consider these characteristics when planning your piece and the room it will sit in. Also think about the frame in relation to the fabric. Is the show wood dark or light? Or will you paint it to work with your fabric choice?

Pattern

There are many pattern styles to consider. There are geometrics, such as spots, stripes, rectangles, triangles and checks. Then there are motifs – patterns made up of repeated images. Motifs might be animals, plants or any other figurative or abstract design.

Perhaps even more so than colour, pattern has a life span, and the popularity of patterns is dictated by the fashion cycle. It's easy to become bored by a particular pattern, so if in doubt, go for a classic. This doesn't have to mean an 'old' pattern, but something solid, well designed and with a print quality to match. Patterns add real personality to a piece of furniture and the room as a whole, so make sure you really love them.

Chaise longue upholstered in patchwork by Like That One.

Top right: Lily chair upholstered by Andrea Mihalik of Wild Chairy.
Right: Butterfly chair designed by Tortie Hoare. Upholstered in leather and Josef Frank linen.

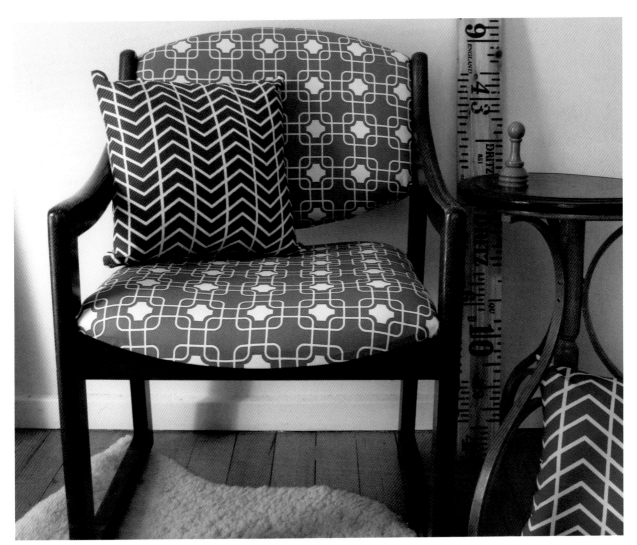

Retro armchair upholstered in Hollywood Trellis fabric by Lisa Barrett for Tango & James.

Think about the size of the pattern in relation to the chair. A small pattern might be lost on a large chair and from a distance will look more like a textured fabric. A large pattern is quite a statement. Obviously this comes down to the individual pattern; it's all about experimentation. Get a sample of the fabric and lay it on the chair. Play around with positioning. It might be that the pattern looks best off-centre rather than bang in the middle.

Take special care when using striped fabric; the eye can be easily drawn to an area that is slightly overstretched and distorted, or piping that doesn't quite line up.

Pattern is not just restricted to flat cotton, but can also be found on deep-pile fabrics or created in the weave. As well as traditional tartans and tweeds, look out for more playful woven yarns.

Texture

Think about how the fabric feels.
Will you actually be able to sit on
the chair for long periods of time?
The fabric on a sofa might be durable,
but does it make you want to sink into
it for an evening? Are you lucky enough
to live in a hot country where you will
only be able to bear the cooling touch
of linen?

Top: Drops chair by Camilla Hounsell Halvorsen.
Bottom: Knit stool by Claire-Anne O'Brien.

Don Rex rocking chair upholstered in eco-wool and upcycled tartan by Flourish and Blume.

Durability

Ercol chair upholstered by Lucy Davidson.

Because of the daily wear on your furniture, upholstery fabrics are generally of a much heavier weight than textiles for clothing or soft furnishings. Even so, they have their own particular levels of durability. Think about where the chair will live. Will it be in the bedroom covered in clothes or jumped on by kids and pets in the living room? Check the fabric's resistance to abrasion and how likely it is to pill or tear.

Where in the room will the piece of furniture sit? Next to the window or by a radiator? Colours will inevitably fade if near a window – and in artificial light, too. Unless you're planning on living in the dark or in a heat-controlled environment, there's not an awful lot you can do to prevent this, apart from take the best care you can of a piece of furniture.

1960s G Plan wing chair in Concourse fabric by Andrew Martin and a leather hide from Halo. Upholstery by Florrie + Bill.

Making fabric

You can print onto fabric, embellish pre-made fabric or even weave your own. When designing fabric, be inspired by what's around you. Think about colour, pattern and scale in relation to your piece and the room it will end up in. Whichever printing technique you use, experiment with materials or play with scale. Be open to ideas, keep a sketchbook and create something unique.

Top: Love London photography by Barbara Chandler,
fabric design and printing by Digitex, upholstered by Urban Upholstery.
Right: Eep and Herds fabrics by Skinny laMinx.

DIGITAL PRINTING

Digital printing is a pain-free and cheaper alternative to screen-printing. A digital printer is essentially the same as your home printer, except it is larger and prints onto fabric. The turnaround is (usually) quick and you can produce designs for a small run – making it possible to create fabric for one chair. You can be as creative as you like in terms of colour and pattern. The range of colours is only limited by the set-up of the supplier. If you like, the pattern can be specific to each panel of your chair. Re-sizing elements of your design and breaking the repeat are also possible, and you should receive samples so you can check the quality before going ahead.

To minimise wasted fabric and save money, produce prints to fit each panel of your chair, for example the inside back and the seat, then organise each panel so they fit together. A good supplier will be able to help you with this.

Birds n Bees. Digitally printed fabric by Timorous Beasties.

White Moth Allover. Digitally printed fabric by Timorous Beasties.

Dandelion screen-printed fabric from St. Judes.

SCREEN-PRINTING

Screen-printing is certainly more hands-on and involved than digital printing. The results are not always perfect, but sometimes the best or most interesting print is the result of a mistake. The screen itself is made from a metal or wooden frame with one side covered in a woven mesh. In its simplest form, a paper stencil is placed between the screen and the fabric, and ink is then pulled across the screen with a squeegee. It will only transfer onto the fabric through the open area of the stencil. More commonly, a photosensitive medium is spread across the mesh and an image is exposed onto it. Once the medium is washed away from the screen, you are left with open areas for the ink to pass through. Every colour in a design requires its own separate screen.

Taking a course in screen-printing is a good idea, even if you intend to print at home. The tips, advice and inspiration you will get from working with other printmakers are invaluable.

If you do go down the home-printing route, everything you need, including the chemicals, can be bought online or from large art suppliers. You'll then need enough space to print, somewhere completely dark for the light-sensitive screen to dry and the correct wattage bulb for exposing the screen. Exposing the screen will be a case of trial and error – as will the printing results themselves. The texture of your fabric and how hard you press or how many pulls of the squeegee you use will all add to the effect of the finished print. It's best to start with a simple design in one colour.

Curiosity Shop. Screen-printed fabric designed by Emily Sutton for St. Judes.

Bird Garden. Screen-printed fabric designed by
Mark Hearld for St. Judes.

Little Animals. Screen-printed fabric designed by Celia Birtwell.

Block-printed fabrics by Jesse Breytenbach.

BLOCK OR LINO PRINTING

A lino print is essentially a step up from the classic potato print. Lino is available as a flat sheet or ready-mounted on a wooden block. The flat sheet option is more suited for a printing press. The latter makes for an easier, more even print if you're printing at home. Lino is suited to line-heavy designs rather than blocks of colour and has a handmade texture and feel. It can be time consuming and possibly painful depending on how intricate your design is and how skillful you are with a lino cutter.

To make a print, transfer the image onto the lino by drawing, tracing or with a photocopy and nail polish remover. Remembering that the image will need to be back to front, photocopy your design, then place it face down onto the lino. With some absorbent paper, dab the back with the nail polish remover to transfer the design.

When it comes to cutting, keep both hands behind the blade. If possible, clamp the lino down so you have more control. Heating the lino will make it easier to cut.

With careful positioning and marking, it is possible to produce repeat patterns. Experiment with different colours by offsetting the lino on the next print. Do check the transparency of the ink and how the colours mix before committing them to your final fabric. If you have a lot of time on your hands and a bit of lino experience, try reduction printing – or suicide printing, as it's better known. The principle is that you only use one block of lino for each colour. To do this, make your first cut and print. Then cut and print again, and so on, and so on. You'll need to plan this method carefully, making registration marks and printing light colours before dark.

STENCILLING

The principle of stencilling is to cut a design in a sheet material such as paper or plastic and apply paint through the cut-out areas. You can transfer paint through these openings by spraying, sponging or brushing, for example.

To allow for repeated use, it's best to cut the stencil design onto plastic. You can buy sturdy plastic that can be put through your home printer – the design is then cut out with a craft knife. A heat pen is also a useful tool. Practise with both before over-cutting or melting your design.

Use spray glue or pins to fix your fabric flat and use the same spray to fix the stencil to the fabric. If you're worried about gluing on the upper side of the fabric, then just tape the stencil in place and take care when applying the paint. Test the stencil and your chosen application method on a scrap piece of fabric first.

EMBELLISHING

Even the most basic sewing techniques can change the feel of a fabric. Try to think beyond the played-out patchwork covers and use the fabric in a different way. Be inventive with cutting and sewing.

APPLIQUÉ

Appliqué, meaning 'to be applied', involves sewing a piece of fabric onto another piece of fabric. It has been around for centuries – but your appliqué designs don't need to look as if they have.

EMBROIDERY

The traditional description of embroidery is the decoration of fabric using a needle and thread. But don't be restricted by your preconceptions – embroidery doesn't need to be twee and floral. Experiment with the materials you have and don't be bound by tradition.

Stencil-printed fabrics by Jesse Breytenbach.

Block chair with machine-embroidered patchwork by Eleanor Young.

Upholstery Techniques

Bommel chair upholstered by MYK.

Slipcovers

You really only need basic sewing skills to make a slipcover. The procedure is pretty simple – or as simple as the chair you are covering. You can make it harder with the addition of fancy pleating or embellishments, but if it is your first attempt, choose a chair with good, clean lines.

Plan the panels that need to fit together. You may need to add a zip or Velcro to the back to make it fit. Pre-wash the fabric to allow for shrinkage.

YOU WILL NEED
- Fabric
- Pins
- Scissors
- Sewing machine
- Tape measure
- Tailor's chalk

TIPS
The slipcover should not be too tight in the areas where the back and the arms meet the seat. There needs to be just that little bit extra that can be tucked in to prevent the seams from ripping when you sit in the chair.

If your chair is an awkward shape, just lay some oversized fabric in place and pin. Remove from the chair, measure the seam allowance and cut.

ARMS

1 Pin some oversized fabric to the outside and inside of the arms, wrong side up. Make sure the fabric is properly tensioned across all faces, but is not too tight, and mark the curve or line of the arm with chalk. Remove from the chair and perfect the line. Add a seam allowance and cut.

2 Use these pieces as a template for the opposite arm, remembering that the fabric needs to be the opposite way. Now bring all the pieces back to the chair and pin in place, wrong side up.

3 Measure the arm borders, add a seam allowance and cut the fabric. Bring the border to the chair and pin in place. Line up the edge of the border with the edge of the inside and outside arms. Pin together. When everything is in place, notch the fabric in a few places just to be extra safe. Remove from the chair.

4 Machine-stitch the arms together so that the tension between the inside arm and seat is correct and not over pulled. Bring back to the chair.

BACK AND SEAT

5 Measure and cut (with seam allowance) your inside back and seat. Place the fabric wrong side facing out on the chair and pin to the bottom of the inside arm and the side of the arm border on the front of the chair. You are now making a three-way seam: one from the arm to the top of the seat, one from the seat top to the bottom of the chair and one from the front of the seat to the back. You'll need to make a few small release cuts to help ease the fabric round the curve of the front of the seat. Bringing these seams together can be fiddly; it might help to sew one seam, bring the cover back to the chair, then mark and sew the next. Remember that the finished seam on the front will be very visible, so make sure it is straight.

6 Measure and cut the fabric for the outside back with a seam allowance. Place the fabrics wrong side up and pin to the inside back and outside arms. If your chair is bigger at the top than it is at the bottom, it's likely you'll need to add a zip on one side of the back.

7 Turn up the hem along the bottom of the chair and pin. Make the drop just a touch longer than the chair itself. Remove from the chair and machine together. If you don't want any visible stitching, use some fusible tape and iron together instead.

1

3

5

2

7

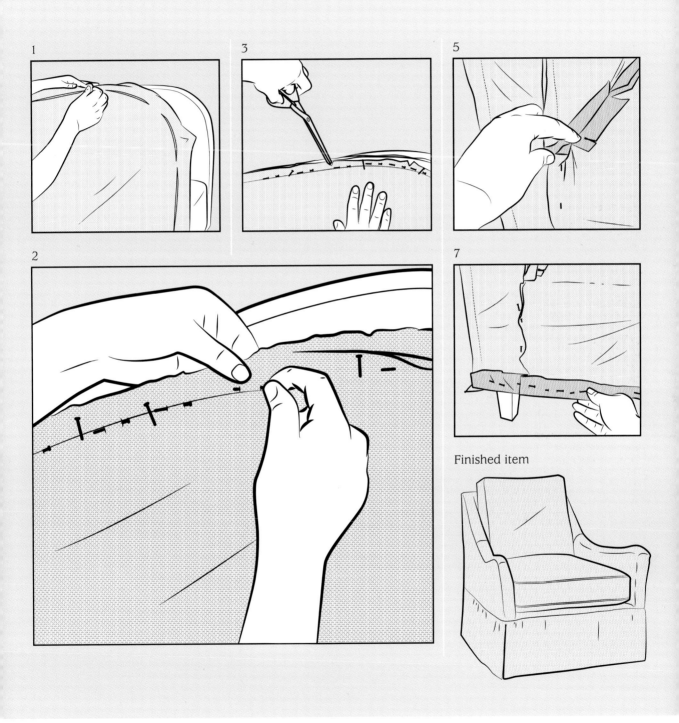

Finished item

Drop-in seat

MODERN TECHNIQUE

Upholstering a drop-in seat is a quick and simple way to update a chair. Depending on the age of the chair or how much time you have, you can opt for either the modern or the traditional technique. Don't be tempted to just throw your new fabric over the old filling, as this will add bulk. With a just a few extra minutes of prep, you can have a brand new seat or even a full set of chairs.

YOU WILL NEED

- Ripping chisel
- Mallet
- Staple remover
- Pincers
- Sandpaper
- Webbing and hessian
- Web strainer
- Foam

- Electric carving knife
- Sheet of plastic
- Spray fabric adhesive
- Polyester wadding
- Tape measure or ruler
- Top cover fabric
- Scissors

- Tailor's chalk
- Tacks
- Hammer
- Staple gun
- Staples
- Calico

1 Rip down your drop-in seat (see page 94). Make sure there are no staples or anything sharp left on the frame that could tear the fabric or your hands. Go over the seat with some sandpaper to soften or remove any loose splinters. Some modern chairs have a solid board base with no webbing. If this is the case with your chair, skip straight to step 2.

If your seat has an open frame, you will need to make a base, which you can either do with a thin piece of wood or using webbing and hessian. If you choose the latter, web across the frame no more than a web-space apart and cover with 12oz hessian (see page 108).

2 Lay the seat onto some foam. Ask your supplier for advice on choosing foam if you are unsure what you need. Draw around the frame with a marker pen. The finished piece of foam should have a slight overhang of about 5mm (¼in) on all sides.

3 Use an electric carving knife to cut the foam. If you have no access to a carving knife or you don't trust your carving skills, ask your supplier to cut the foam for you.

4 Working in a well-ventilated area, place the seat on a sheet of plastic and spray the top of the seat and the foam with fabric adhesive. Wait a minute or so, then stick the seat onto the foam (not the other way around) – it's easier to position this way. Now, either cover the seat with polyester and follow with the top cover, or add some calico strips to the edges for strength (see Tips on page 73).

5 Cover the seat in a layer of polyester wadding, making sure it doesn't extend down over the edges. Measure the seat and cut your top cover with about 5cm (2in) extra on all sides. This will give you something to pull on and make the fabric easier to position. Lay the fabric over the seat, making sure that the threads are in line with the seat edge for that professional look. This is especially important if you are working with a striped fabric. For greater accuracy, mark the front and back centres of the seat and fabric with tailor's chalk. Turn the seat onto its side with the front side facing up. Line up the centre marks.

6 Temporary tack the fabric in the middle on the underside of the seat. Turn the frame around to the opposite side, lining up the centre marks. Smooth the fabric from the bottom to the top with one hand and gently pull it over the edge and under the seat with your other hand. You should be applying slight pressure to crush the edges of the foam and create a rounded edge. Again, temporary tack the fabric in place on the underside of the seat.

7 Repeat step 6 on the remaining two sides. Keep checking how uniform the top cover is looking. When you are happy with the roundness of the edges and your cover is straight, permanently fix the fabric in place, stopping just short of the corners. If you want your corners to be sharp and square, finish with a single corner. For a more rounded finish go for a double (see page 152). When complete, trim away any excess fabric.

8 Finish with some calico tacked or stapled onto the underside of the seat (tacks look more professional).

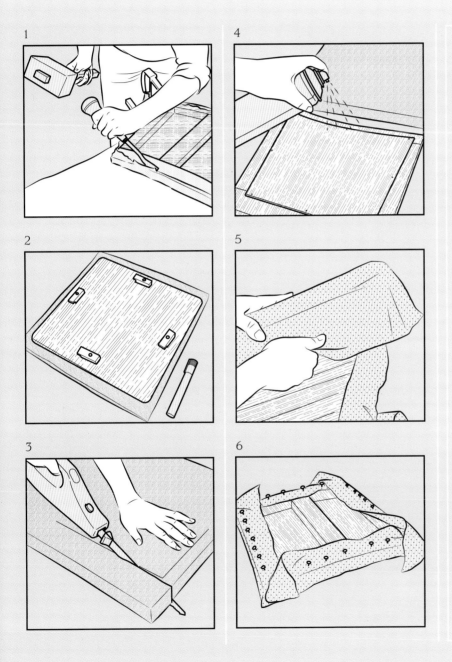

1

2

3

4

5

6

TIPS

After step 4, when the foam is glued to the seat, you can reinforce your edges using calico strips. This will also help you create a good shape before adding your top cover. This technique only works if you have a flat drop-in seat, as you need to apply equal pressure on all sides.

1 Cut four strips of calico, equal in length to the edges of the foam. Measure the edge and quarter of the top and bottom for your width. Lay one piece of calico on top of the foam and spray both with adhesive. Wait a minute or so, then stick them together.

2 Turn the seat over so that the foam is now facing the table. Spray more adhesive onto the calico flap, wait a minute, then, while applying some pressure to the frame edge, pull the calico onto the underside of the seat. The goal is to create an even, smooth edge. Continue this process on all sides, then return to step 5 in the main instuctions.

Drop-in seat

TRADITIONAL TECHNIQUE

YOU WILL NEED

- Ripping chisel
- Mallet
- Staple remover
- Pincers
- Sandpaper
- G-clamp
- Webbing and hessian
- Web strainer
- Curved needle

- Nylon thread
- Hair
- Tape measure or ruler
- Calico
- Scissors
- Tacks
- Hammer
- Skin wadding
- Top cover fabric

1 Once ripped down and sanded (see page 72, step 1), clamp the seat to a sturdy table. The clamp will stop the seat from moving around while you strain the webbing. Web no more than a web-space apart and cover with 12oz hessian (see page 108). Using a curved needle, make evenly-spaced bridle ties with nylon thread following the line of the seat (see page 110).

2 Tease the hair and scoop under the ties, re-teasing as you go. Incorrect scooping could make the hair lumpy again, so you need to keep checking. When you are sure the coverage is even, tuck any stray hair under itself at the edges. Any hair overhang will just add extra bulk to the sides of the seat. The thickness of the hair should be about 4cm (1½in).

3 Measure from the underside of the frame on one side to the underside on the other, adding approximately 5cm (2in) to this measurement on all sides. Cut out the calico. Temporary tack the calico to the underside of the seat.

4 Turn the frame around to the opposite side and with one hand smooth the calico from the bottom to the top while pulling over the edge and under the seat with the other hand. Temporary tack the calico in place. (The smoothing, holding and tacking technique is tricky but will become easier with practice.) Repeat on the remaining two sides. Keep checking to make sure your thread lines are straight and even.

5 When you are happy with the firmness and evenness of the calico, permanently tack on the edges, stopping short of the corners. The calico should be quite tight and unpinchable. Finish with a single corner (see page 152).

6 Cover with a layer of skin wadding, again making sure not to cover the edges of the seat. (The skin wadding prevents hair from coming up through the fabric.) Repeat steps 3 and 4 with your top fabric. When complete, trim away any excess fabric.

7 Apply some bottom cloth to the underside of the seat, finishing with a neat row of tacks. To do this, turn the seat over and measure and cut some calico. Fold under on one edge and temporary tack in place.

8 Pull to the opposite side and temporary tack. Repeat with the remaining two sides. When you're happy with the positioning, permanently tack the fabric.

1

2

5

6

7

Finished item

Upholstered screen

MAKING A SCREEN FRAME

The following instructions show you how to make a screen in the most basic way possible. However, you'll still need to be as precise as you can. You may yawn when you hear 'measure twice, cut once'... but ignore at your peril!

If you already have a screen that simply needs a new look, turn to page 78.

YOU WILL NEED

- 5 × 2.5cm (2 × 1in) lengths of PAR (planed all round) wood, at least as long as you want your frame to be tall
- Tape measure
- G-clamps
- Try square (or a saw with 90-degree markings)
- Pencil
- Saw
- Sandpaper and block
- Drill with countersink
- Wood glue
- Screws

TIPS
Some saws show 45 and 90 degrees as part of the handle and saw-edge relationship. You can push the edge of the handle to the side of the wood and the top of the saw will be at 90 degrees to the edge.

1 These instructions are for a three-panel screen, with each panel shown here being 180cm (70in) high and 60cm (24in) wide. The frame is made of PAR wood, which is planed smooth and is therefore easier to work with and unlikely to snag any fillings or fabrics. Once you've worked out all your measurements, you can either cut the wood yourself or get the timber merchant to cut it for you (in which case, go to step 4).

2 To cut and drill the uprights: begin by selecting the straightest lengths of wood; some can bow slightly in the planing process. Clamp six lengths together using at least two clamps. Using your try square or the edge of your saw (if it has 90-degree markings, see Tips above) mark a straight line across all lengths and down the sides.

3 Saw along the line. You must keep checking that you are also following the line down the sides of the wood as well as across the top – this will ensure a straight cut edge. Mark 180cm (70in) from this cut and repeat the process. If you've cut correctly you should now have six 180cm (70in) lengths with straight edges. Lightly sand where you've cut to remove any splinters.

4 While your lengths are still clamped together, mark out the positioning of the crossrails on all sides of the wood. This example has four crossrails on each frame. Pre-drill the screw holes, keeping them as close to the centre of the wood as possible to avoid splitting. Make two holes for each crossrail.

5 Cutting the crossrails: this example has 12. As before, clamp six lengths together, square off the ends and cut to your desired lengths. In this case, the crossrails need to be 50cm (19½in) in length; 60cm (23½in) minus the width of the uprights (5 × 5/2 × 2in cm).

6 Start assembling the frames. Lay some offcuts of wood on the floor to raise the frame and make it easier to work with and to keep the frame from being glued to the floor. Start by attaching the top and bottom crossrails. Squeeze some glue onto the end of the rail and some onto the upright, then bring them together – wiggle the pieces together to free any air bubbles and evenly disperse the glue.

7 While holding the pieces in place and constantly checking that the top of the rail is aligned to the top of the upright, screw them together. When the top and bottom rails are tightly screwed, fix the two inner rails. Make sure to fix both rails on one side then fix both on the other. Repeat the process for the remaining frames and let them dry flat.

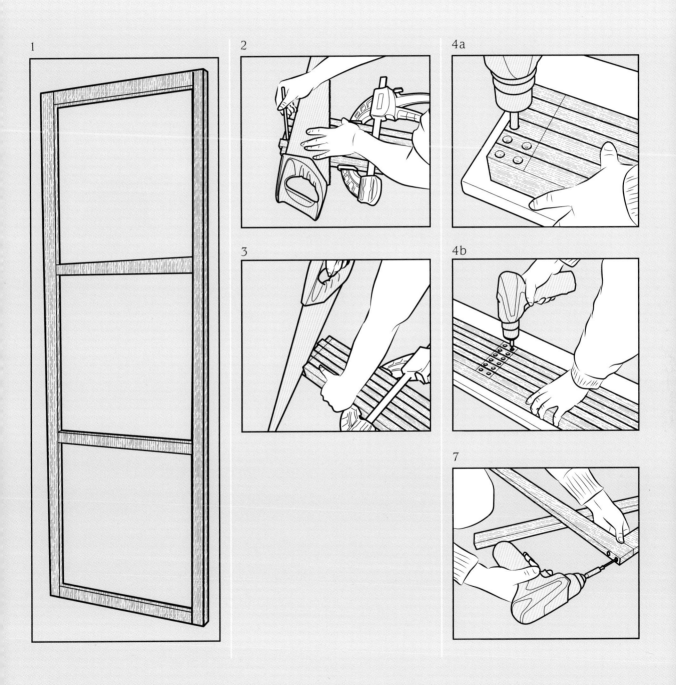

Upholstered screen

UPHOLSTERING THE FRAME

YOU WILL NEED

- 7oz hessian (quantity will depend on your frame size)
- Scissors
- Tacks
- Hammer
- Staple gun
- Staples

- Polyester wadding (quantity will vary)
- Top cover fabric
- Trimming, gimp or braid
- Hot glue gun
- Hinges
- Feet glides (optional)

TIPS

In step 1, what you're trying to achieve is a flat surface for the wadding and top cover fabric to lie on. You could make the whole frame out of a solid piece of wood, as long as you had no intention of ever moving it! The materials you decide to use will come down to money and time. Hessian, calico, or even stretched paper – it's really up to you.

1 With the frame on the floor, measure out the hessian with a slight overhang. Fold under and temporary tack. Stretch out the hessian to the opposite edge – but not so much that you distort the frame. Again, fold under and temporary tack. Repeat on the remaining two sides, working from one side to the other. When you are happy with the positioning, permanently staple in place.

2 Cover the hessian in polyester wadding and staple on the edge of the frame. You'll only need a few staples on each edge, as the fabric will eventually hold the wadding in place. Remove any polyester overhang from the edges of the screen.

3 Measure and cut the top cover fabric with enough extra on each side for pulling. Position the fabric and temporary tack it on the edges of the frame. Remember to tack from one side to the other, keeping the fabric taut. When you are happy with the positioning, permanently staple in place.

4 Repeat steps 1 and 2 on the reverse of the screen, finishing with single pleats at the corners facing away from you. In other words, the shadow of the single fold faces the ceiling or the floor.

5 Trim the waste fabric as close to the middle of the edge of the frame as possible. This example is finished using wide trim attached with a combination of staples and hot glue. Secure one end of the trimming with some staples on the underside of the frame. Hot glue the trim around the frame and finish by stapling on the underside.

6 Finally, attach the hinges, taking care not to tear your fabric. You can also fix some feet glides to the bottom at this stage if you prefer to have the screen raised off the floor.

1

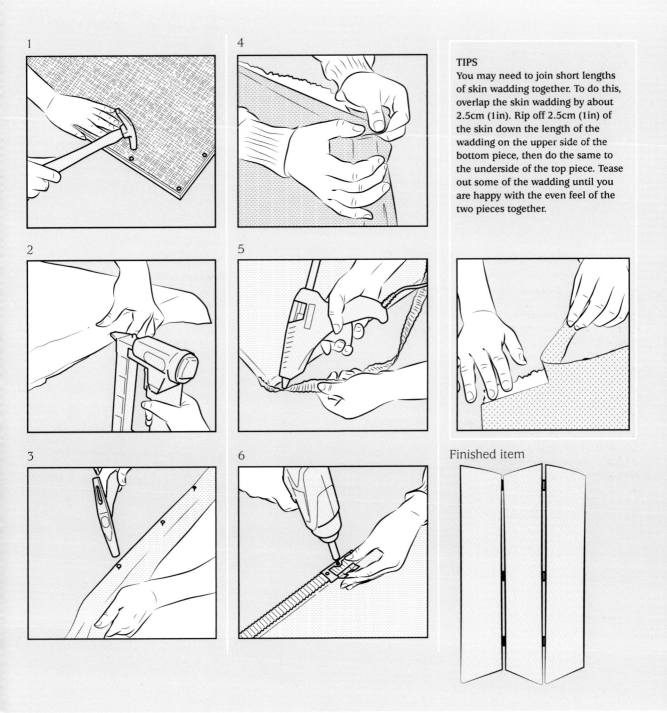

2

3

4

5

6

TIPS
You may need to join short lengths of skin wadding together. To do this, overlap the skin wadding by about 2.5cm (1in). Rip off 2.5cm (1in) of the skin down the length of the wadding on the upper side of the bottom piece, then do the same to the underside of the top piece. Tease out some of the wadding until you are happy with the even feel of the two pieces together.

Finished item

Piped box cushion

Many chairs and sofas have separate cushions that will also need covering, or perhaps you have a bench you'd like to make more comfortable. Whichever, being able to make a box cushion is a handy skill to have.

YOU WILL NEED
- Foam cushion form
- Tape measure
- Piping cord (pre-shrunk or washed)
- Top cover fabric
- Scissors
- Tailor's chalk
- Sewing machine with a piping foot
- Sewing thread
- Stockinette or polyester wadding
- Spray adhesive

TIPS
For a quick piping join: make sure there is an overlap of piping fabric. Cut the two pieces of cord together so that both ends meet. Tuck one end of covered piping inside the other. Fold over the end of the overlapping piece. Hold tightly together and continue to sew the piping to the main piece of fabric.

1 Decide on your cushion size: measure the circumference of your cushion and multiply this by two. Make up some piping for this amount plus about 10–15cm (4–6in) for joining. (See page 160 for more about piping.)

2 Cut the top and bottom pieces of fabric, adding a 1.5cm (½in) seam allowance to all sides. Mark the centre points on both pieces.

3 Lay the piping on the right side of the top piece of fabric. The cord should be facing into the cushion and the cut edge lined up with the fabric edge. Keep any of the joins in the piping towards the back of the cushion where they will be out of sight. Leaving about 6cm (2½in) of piping free, backstitch for a few stitches then machine stitch the piping and fabric together. Stop just short of the corner of the cushion. Mark the piping 1.5cm (½in) back from the edge. Then mark again 5mm (¼in) between you and the first mark.

4 Cut at these points just up to the stitched line and continue sewing. When you reach the corner, keep the needle in the fabric and lift the foot. Turn the fabric, lower the foot and continue sewing. If there are any curves in your cushion, make release cuts to help ease the piping round the curve.

5 To join the piping, stop short of finishing by about 6cm (2½in). Lay both ends of piping over each other and mark a 4cm (1½in) overlap. (This is dependent on your piping width also being 4cm/1½in.) Cut the overlapped piece of piping at this mark.

6 Open out both pieces of piping to expose the cord. Bring the two right sides of piping fabric together. Line the top corner of the right-hand piece up with the bottom corner of the left-hand piece and pin. Line the end edge of the right-hand piece up with the bottom edge of the left-hand piece and pin.

7 Sew across the diagonal starting from the bottom corner of the right-hand piece to the top corner of the left-hand piece. Trim the excess about 5mm (¼in) from the sewn line. Open out and flatten.

8 Lay the stitched piping flat against the top piece of fabric. Lay the two pieces of piping cord next to each other. Cut the piping together so that the two ends butt together.

9 Cut out the border piece of fabric, adding a 1.5cm (½in) seam allowance at top and bottom and on both ends. If your cushion is quite large and you need to cut more than one length for your border,

make sure to add a seam allowance to each end. Sew the border lengths together with a 1.5cm (½in) seam allowance, open out the seam and press. Mark the centre points on the top and bottom of the border to coincide with the marks you made on the top and bottom pieces.

10 Line up a mark on the border with a mark on the top fabric with right sides facing. Pin together at this point then continue pinning all the edges. Sew the border to the top fabric.

11 Keeping the sewn pieces inside out, place the foam cushion form inside to check the fit. Then lay the bottom fabric piece on the foam (wrong side out). Make sure the corners are aligned and pin to the border, leaving an opening to enable you to remove the foam. Now sew the bottom piece to the border, leaving an opening to insert the foam cushion form. Turn right side out.

12 Cover the foam cushion in either stockinette or polyester wadding. The latter will give a softer feel and appearance. Cut to size and use spray adhesive to close the edges. When dry, work the foam cushion form into the cover.

13 Close the opening with a slip stitch (see page 114).

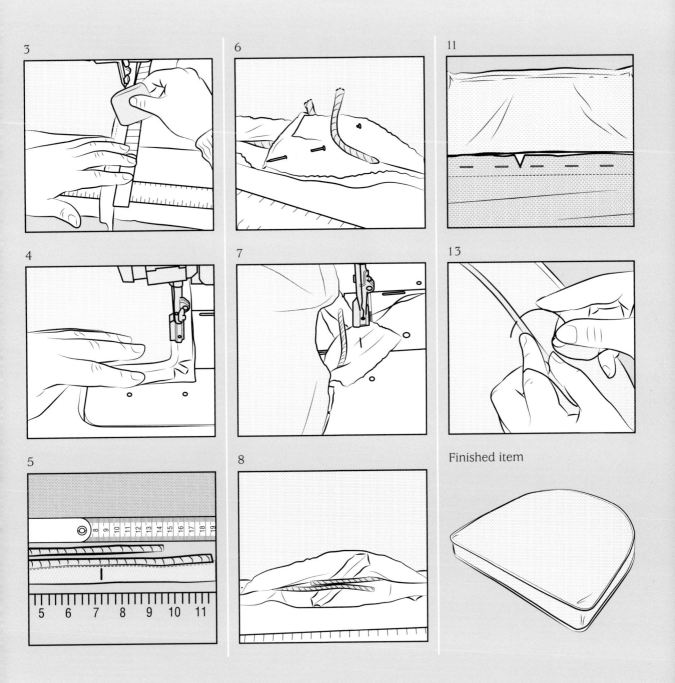

3

4

5

6

7

8

11

13

Finished item

Adding a zip

There are many ways to add a zip, in this example I will put the zip into its own border, then attach this to the front cushion border. Your zip can run the length of the cushion and come slightly round the sides for easy cushion insertion, but I like to have the zip run on one side just short of the edges. It's obviously harder to get the filling in, but I prefer the look.

YOU WILL NEED
- Standard zip
- Cushion
- Tape measure
- Scissors
- Sewing machine
- Seam ripper

1 Work out how long you want your finished zip to be. I suggest making it start and finish a couple of centimetres in from the edges on one side. Cut a zip slightly longer than you need it to be. Then cut the zip panel. This needs to be the length of your finished zip, plus 3cm (1in) seam allowance on the length (1.5cm/½in for both ends) and the height of your border plus 6cm (2in) seam allowance (1.5cm/½in for the top and bottom plus 1.5cm/½in for each side of the zip). Measure the half line down the length of your fabric and cut. Make sure you are incredibly accurate with your cutting! (See Tips).

2 Using some contrasting colour thread and a long stitch length on your machine, sew the lengths back together right sides facing with a 1.5cm (½in) seam allowance. Iron the seam open flat on the wrong side.

3 Place your closed zip with the teeth facing down and central to the seam. Pin and hand tack on either side of the teeth.

4 Turn over so the right side of the fabric is facing up. Sew down each side of the seam. Using a seam ripper, take out the stitches covering the teeth from step 2. Also remove the hand tacking.

5 Measure and cut a front border piece. This is the circumference of your cushion plus a 3cm (1in) seam allowance (that's 1.5cm/½in for both ends and top and bottom) minus the length of your finished zip. Notch the centre marks on the top and bottom and line up with the centre notches on your top cushion panel. Sew the border to the bottom section, stopping short of the ends.

6 Trim any excess zip to the edges of the zip border. Notch the centre marks on your zip border and match to the centre notch on your top cushion panel. Machine in place, stopping just short of the ends.

7 Bring the ends of your front border and zip border together with the right sides facing. Machine them together with a 1.5cm (½in) seam allowance.

8 Turn over so that the right sides are facing up and machine a top stitch. Repeat on the opposite end. Sew the complete border to the top cushion panel.

9 Open the zip, line up the centre notches on the border with the centre notches on the bottom cushion panel and machine. Turn right side out and insert the cushion.

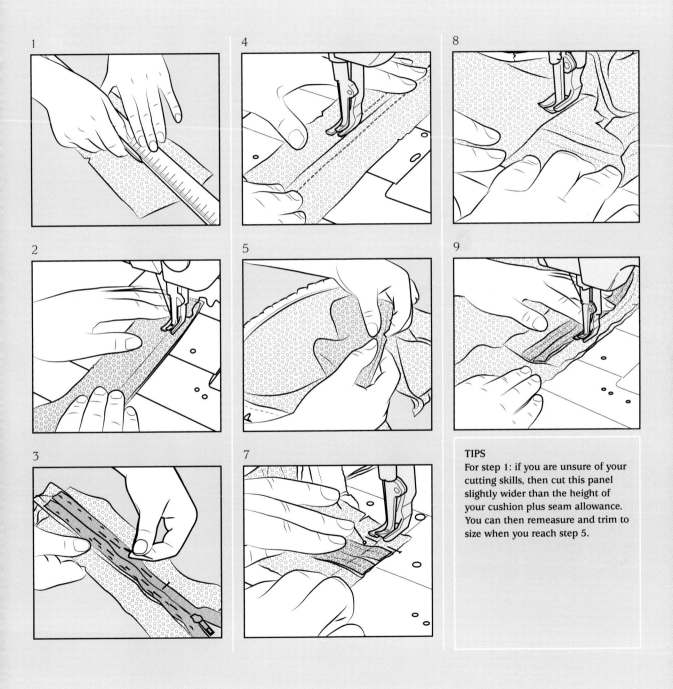

1

2

3

4

5

7

8

9

TIPS
For step 1: if you are unsure of your cutting skills, then cut this panel slightly wider than the height of your cushion plus seam allowance. You can then remeasure and trim to size when you reach step 5.

Seams & stitching

Much mid-century and modern upholstery is predominantly sewing based.
Many sofas and day beds are made up of a series of cushions often supported
by rubber webbing. Some modern furniture is produced in component
parts – the upholstery machined entirely and simply slipped over each
part individually.

If cushion making and sewing is a large part of your work, try to think beyond
the plain old seam. A piped seam is strong and can also be used to add a
contrasting colour or to define a shape. But a top stitch, perhaps with an
interesting thread, can also be durable with a decorative finish.

Plain seam

As plain as they come! This is the
most commonly-used type of seam.

1 Machine fabric right sides together
with a 1.5cm (½in) seam allowance.

Flat fell seam

Usually used to strengthen a seam on
fabrics such as denim. The seam can
sometimes get bulky, so test with your
fabric first.

1 Machine fabric right sides together
with a 1.5cm (½in) seam allowance.

2 Press open the seam.

3 Trim one side of the seam allowance
back by half.

4 Fold the longer edge over and under
the shorter edge.

5 Press and machine close to the fold.

Machined top stitch

1 Machine fabric right sides together
with a 1.5cm (½in) seam allowance.

2 On the wrong side, press the
seam allowance together to one side.

3 Machine both together close to
the fold.

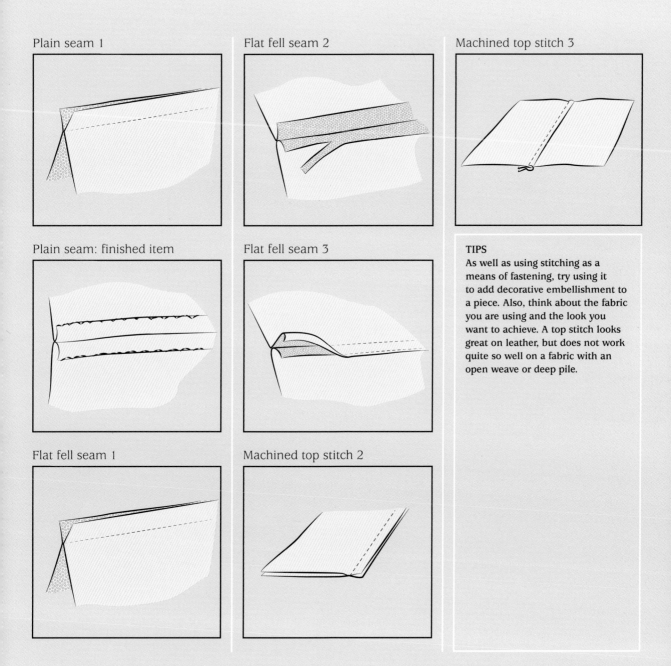

Plain seam 1

Flat fell seam 2

Machined top stitch 3

Plain seam: finished item

Flat fell seam 3

TIPS
As well as using stitching as a
means of fastening, try using it
to add decorative embellishment to
a piece. Also, think about the fabric
you are using and the look you
want to achieve. A top stitch looks
great on leather, but does not work
quite so well on a fabric with an
open weave or deep pile.

Flat fell seam 1

Machined top stitch 2

Seams & stitching

Plain seam sewn through

I've seen this used on the edges of simple unbordered cushions and I like the effect it gives. It also works well on slightly thicker fabrics.

1 Place the fabric with right sides together and sew roughly 5mm (¼in) from the edge.

2 Turn the fabric so that the wrong sides are now facing each other.

3 Sew again about 1cm (½in) in from the edge.

Overlocking

Open ends of fabric can be overlocked to minimise the risk of fraying. Overlocking machines are made with various thread formations; three-thread overlocking is used for sewing pintucks, creating narrow rolled hems, finishing fabric edges, decorative edging and seaming knit or woven fabrics. Four-thread overlocking is used for decorative edging and finishing, seaming high-stress areas and mock safety stitches that create extra strength while retaining flexibility.

If you do not have an overlocking machine or a specialist foot attachment for your sewing machine, choose the zigzag setting and run along the edges of the fabric.

Blanket stitch

The blanket stitch has many uses in upholstery. Often it's a stitch that's hidden from sight, for example when sewing hessian to a spring unit.

1 Start with a slip knot and sew to the right.

2 Pass the needle down through the fabric and bring back through the thread. Pull the thread to the right. (If attaching hessian to a spring unit, make sure the needle passes through the hessian and around the edge of the spring unit.)

3 Repeat steps 1 and 2. If attaching hessian to a spring unit then space each stitch about 2.5cm (1in) apart.

Plain seam sewn through 1

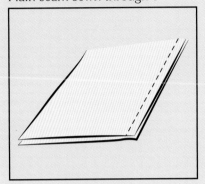

Plain seam sewn through 2

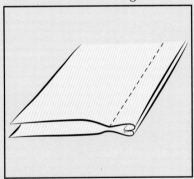

Plain seam sewn through 3

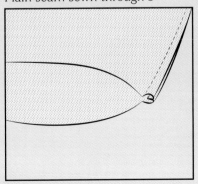

Overlocking: three thread

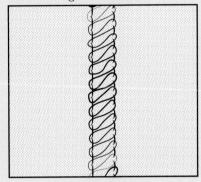

Overlocking: four thread

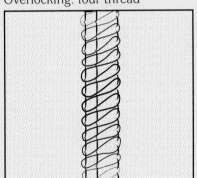

Blanket stitch 1

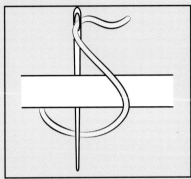

Blanket stitch 2

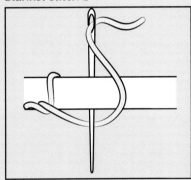

Blanket stitch 3

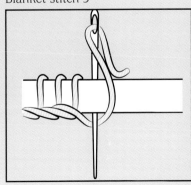

Eleanor Young

Eleanor is a textile designer and upholsterer based in Glasgow, Scotland. She studied at the Glasgow School of Art, specialising in embroidered textiles for furnishings. During her final year she took an evening upholstery class and soon became hooked. 'I felt very strongly that in order to become a better designer I needed to get some hands-on experience of working with fabrics in this way.' After graduating in 2007, Eleanor continued with the evening classes and hasn't looked back. In 2009 she started her company, Fun Makes Good.

FOR TUTORIALS
Cleaning varnished chairs: page 96
Foam: page 132

AFTER

It is always exciting to embark on a new project as I have found no two chairs and commissions are the same. I am constantly learning and honing my skills, which in turn is helping to inform my designs and helps to evolve my style and techniques

CHAIR STYLE
Mid-century Scandinavian Boomerang chairs by Slagelse Møbelvaerk.

FABRIC USED
Sections of the original black vinyl and new sections of coloured upholstery vinyl.

ORIGINAL STATE
Structurally, the chairs were in great condition. Some of the seats had puncture holes in the vinyl and some had slight tears.

CHANGES MADE
The seats were removed and the frames were cleaned. The seats were ripped down and the fillings were replaced.

TIME SPENT
The project took a couple of weeks from the start of the commission – agreeing on designs, sourcing materials, etc. – through to design and completion.

The use of strong graphic shapes runs through much of Eleanor's work, and it's those shapes and the bold use of colour that really complement these chairs – the flipping of the patterns adding that extra touch of interest. For a truly great outcome for any project there needs to be a design process. Eleanor's approach is a perfect example of this process at work: client needs, research, inspiration, ideas and development.

She was asked to create something special for a set of chairs in her signature geometric style. The project: a set of six Boomerang chairs from the Danish furniture producer Slagelse Møbelvaerk. It was agreed that a strong, bold design would be needed to complement the structural 'boomerang' curves and lines. The client also wanted to incorporate the

original black vinyl in some way. While thinking through initial ideas and researching, a painting by the Hungarian artist László Moholy-Nagy came to mind. His use of intersecting lines and shapes became the inspiration and starting point for Eleanor's sketches and design progression. She also kept in mind that the final design should not detract from the chairs themselves. Once the pattern had been developed, panels were interchanged colour wise, and the design flipped from chair to chair.

The frames were in perfect condition and only needed a clean up once the seats were removed. The seat base and the old vinyl coverings were saved. A new foam pad and a layer of wadding was added to each seat. A mixture of coloured vinyls were chosen to sit alongside the original black, some with subtle textures to give depth to the designs. Eleanor was surprised at how malleable and easy to work with the vinyl was. Not surprisingly, once completed, Eleanor found it hard to give the chairs back!

Patrick Feist

Patrick is a salvager, an artist and a craftsman, a collector of beautiful old junk who turns discarded furniture into unique and appealing pieces. A man after my own heart. What I think separates Patrick from many other furniture recyclers is his eye for design. This, combined with his skill as a craftsman and exploratory nature, has led to some unexpected and beautiful work. He lives in Brooklyn, New York.

FOR TUTORIALS
Lashing the springs: page 122
Tufting: page 168
Webbing a seat: page 108

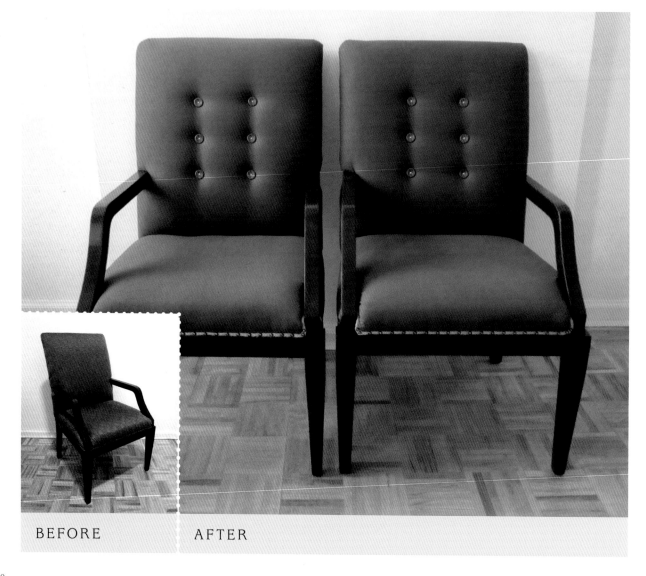

BEFORE   AFTER

What struck me about Patrick's chairs is his use of materials, the way he showcases the hidden and unexpected. With this pair, he's used a combination of burlap and twines that you'd usually only see when ripping down a chair, and the buttons used look more like they should be adorning a jacket than decorating a piece of furniture. Even though there is a rough, feedsack quality to the burlap, the overall look is pretty smart. The colours and the finishing are all perfect.

While sifting through a fabric warehouse, Patrick found a large roll of burlap tucked away in an obscure corner. He then came across a spool of jute rope buried in a back shelf of a trim store. 'That's when I realised I could take those internal elements and bring them to the surface, and that is when I decided on the new look for this set of chairs.'

The chairs were bought from a used office furniture store, a bargain at $40. As you'd expect from a couple of old chairs, they had surface abrasions and patches of water damage. The upholstery was sagging and torn in places – they needed a complete overhaul.

Once the wood work had been touched up, Patrick tightened the webbing and began positioning the springs. As is often the case, lashing the springs was the biggest hurdle. He found that knotting

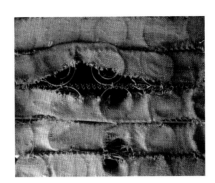

> I've always been amazed at how beautiful an old chair is under the surface. I would strip off upholstery and stuffings and think, 'This old burlap and twine looks great. Why not leave it all exposed?'

each spring as he went worked OK for the first couple, but as he progressed the springs became more and more out of place. He eventually opted for simply winding the twine around each spring, correcting the tension and temporary tacking to the frame on each side.

He then hammered the tacks home and ran some plain lashing across to the top, knotting each spring in place. When the springs were hessian covered, he reworked the old stuffings with some new and tied down. The canvas was then stretched, tacked and finished with jute trim and brass tacks. The back was buttoned to complete the look. Bottom cloth and new metal glides were added to the base and feet.

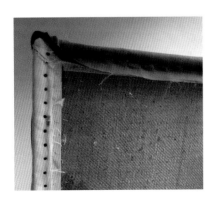

CHAIR STYLE
A variation of the Parsons-style armchair.

FABRIC USED
Medium-weight cotton canvas in granite grey and raw burlap from Mood Fabrics. Jute trim and leather buttons from MJ Trimmings. Antiqued brass tacks from diyupholsterysupply.com

ORIGINAL STATE
The frame had surface abrasions, water staining and loss of finish and colour in areas. The upholstery was faded and stained with frayed patches. The piping trim was loose throughout and pulling away from the frame in areas. The fabric on the back of the chairs was sagging badly, and the bottom lining was torn and hanging down from under the seats.

CHANGES MADE
A complete overhaul. Re-lashing springs. Re-working and addition of stuffing to get the shape back. Clean up of the frame. Re-cover and embellishments.

TIME SPENT
About four days in total, including sourcing materials and learning to re-spring the seats.

Salvaging

Finding and restoring your own furniture is so rewarding. You know that it will have a place with you forever and you'll have the skills to update it whenever you feel the urge. This is surely preferable to having to replace cheap furniture every time something breaks or goes out of fashion. There are many ways to buy second-hand or pick up pieces that have been thrown out – arm yourself with as much information as you can about what to look for and how to get it.

Armchair upholstered in Florence Broadhurst's Japanese Floral fabic and red eco-wool by Flourish and Blume.

WHAT TO LOOK FOR

It's important to be able to assess the general state of an item and how much work will be needed to make it useable – and, of course, beautiful. If it's falling apart with legs missing, then you know you have a whole lot of work ahead. Some ailments aren't quite as obvious though, so here are a few things to look out for when searching for that future heirloom.

THE UPHOLSTERY

One of the most important parts of a chair is the seat. In an ideal world you would want this to be able to take your weight for many years to come. After pressing your hand on the seat to feel for any dips, turn the chair over. Are the webs loose and the springs starting to sag below the frame? If they are, you will need to strip the chair back, re-web, re-spring, stuff and cover. If you're lucky and it's all intact, take the time to have a good feel around. Squeeze the arms and the back. Is the stuffing moving around inside? Or can you actually feel the frame through the layers of upholstery?

THE FRAME

Then there's the frame itself. The odd knock or discolouration can usually be dealt with pretty easily, but splits in the wood or other signs of water damage are not good signs. If there is any obvious water damage to the frame, then it's likely the upholstery is not in great shape either. Hopefully there will be the obvious water stains to give it away – if not, then just smell it! Are there any signs of woodworm or chipping veneer? Is the chair made up of cane work that's littered with holes? If you intend to have veneer or cane work fixed, be aware that these are jobs for professionals and that alone might add a few noughts to your budget. What state are the castors in? How many are left and are they antique? Ask yourself whether you want to be searching for similarly old castors or might prefer to have the originals restored – or will you be happy with brand new replacements at a fraction of the cost?

Wooden electrical spool converted into an ottoman by Shelly Miller Leer.

Reclaimed table and chairs upholstered in bespoke origami-inspired patchworks by Eleanor Young.

BUYING

There are many ways to buy second-hand furniture. Online, auctions, carboot sales and so on all have their good and bad points. If you're looking for something in particular, consider carrying samples of your fabric and trimmings with you at all times, or at the very least, a tape measure. The most important piece of information to have with you is your front door measurement.

BUYING ONLINE

Obviously the biggest drawback to online buying (from sites such as eBay and craigslist) is that you can't actually sit in the chair or have a good feel around. You have to rely on the seller's description, which can sometimes be vague. Of course you can ask questions, but whether a chair is comfortable or not is pretty subjective. However, it's possible to pick up some great pieces. It's easy to fall in love online, so get as much information in advance as possible. An obvious advantage of online auctions is that you can sometimes get a really good deal. If you're lucky, you might be the only one interested in that stain-covered wingback…

AUCTION HOUSES

As with online auctions, it could be that you're the only one bidding on a piece, in which case it could be yours for next to nothing. An advantage of a live auction is that you get the chance to sit in a chair, turn it over and have a proper feel around. Remember that the auctioneers have to take their cut, so be aware when you're bidding that you'll have to add a percentage of the selling price on to your final bid.

CARBOOT SALES

Carboot sales are great because not only are the sellers at hand to answer your questions, but they're also not normally salesmen by trade – which in many cases means that the bartering process is easier.

Ripping down

As the name suggests, this technique involves ripping the upholstery from the frame. In reality though, outer fabrics and fillings will usually come away quite easily and cleanly, and care must be taken not to damage the frame. Go carefully and patiently; it might be that the upholstery is the only thing holding the chair together.

Keep a photographic record of every layer you remove. This will help you think ahead and be aware of what fixes to what – sometimes a bare frame can be quite daunting. Even though this stage can be dirty and boring, it's essential for gaining insight into how to put the upholstery back together again. There may be some awkward shapes or cushions that you want to copy, so keep anything that might be useful to create a template from.

> **TIPS**
> It might be that the only thing wrong with the chair is that the webbing has fallen through, so salvaging as much of the original upholstery as possible can be a money-saving and eco-friendly thing to do, if it's in fairly good condition. However, do make sure it's free from vermin.

YOU WILL NEED
- Facemask
- Ripping chisel
- Mallet
- G-clamp
- Pincers
- Staple remover or flat-head screwdriver
- Sandpaper
- Scissors

1 Make sure you are in a well-ventilated area – outside is usually best. Chairs are often filled with years of dust, or worse, depending on where you find them. Ripping down is not particularly glamorous unless you stumble on the odd bit of loose change. Generally, though, it's just dust – so dress down and wear a facemask.

2 The quickest way to remove a traditionally stuffed seat is to cut the stuffing ties, the top stitching and then the blind. Use the ripping chisel to remove the tacks along the seat edge and simply lift off.

3 When you reach the frame, remove any tacks with your ripping chisel and mallet. Work in the direction of the grain so as not to chip the wood. If you're ripping down a drop-in seat (see page 72), clamp the seat to a sturdy table.

4 Remove any staples by pushing the staple remover under the staple and pushing down. If you prefer, you can also use a mallet with the staple remover in the same way as a ripping chisel. Use the pincers to remove any staples that have broken. If you don't have a staple remover, you can use a flat-head screwdriver.

5 When all you have in front of you is a bare frame, sand any rough areas and inspect for any maintenance that needs to be carried out. Are there any loose joints? Signs of woodworm? Perhaps there are gaping holes left by years of tacking that need to be filled. These will all need to be dealt with before you go to the effort of upholstering. (See page 98 for more about strengthening a frame.)

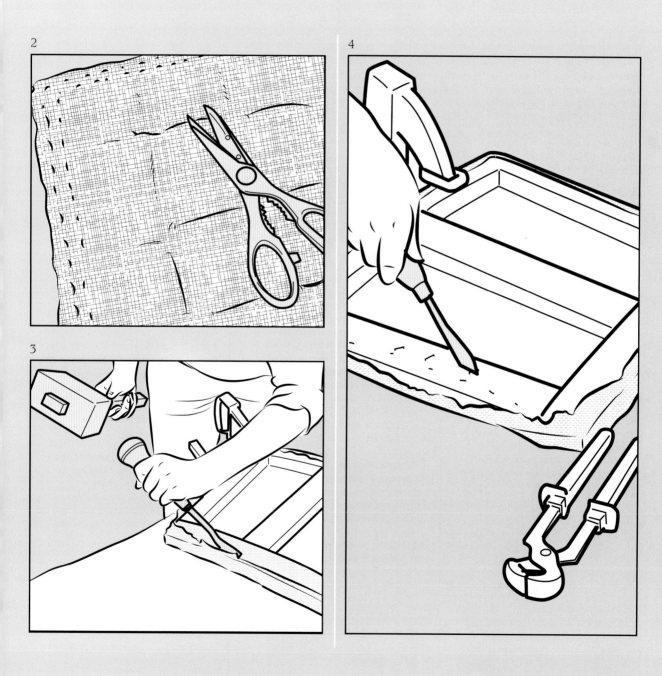

Stripping & cleaning

If you have a chair that is in bad condition with chipped or peeling paint, while your ideal chair has a sleek, smooth frame, then you'll need to invest some time in stripping. Always read the manufacturer's instructions on the paint stripper in case they differ from the directions given here, and make sure that you and your workspace are protected.

Stripping a wooden frame

YOU WILL NEED
- Newspaper or dustsheet
- Gloves
- Eye protection
- Facemask
- Paint stripper
- Paint bucket
- Old paintbrush
- Scraper
- Coarse-grade wire wool
- Old scissors for cutting the wire wool
- Bicarbonate of soda
- Fine-grade sandpaper

1 Prepare your workspace by laying down plenty of newspaper or a dustsheet. Wearing gloves, eye protection and a facemask, pour some stripper into a paint bucket. Read the manufacturer's instructions to check how much stripper to use.

2 With an old paintbrush, slap the stripper over the frame – try not to drag it. Keep it thick and don't let it dry out. If you see patches drying out, add a little extra. Leave for about 15 minutes. After only a few minutes, you'll see the original paint start to bubble, but don't be tempted to start scraping. Be patient and let the stripper do its work.

3 Scrape in the direction of the grain and wipe the spent stripper onto some newspaper. When you have removed most of the excess paint, rub with wire wool in the direction of the grain. Use small pieces and keep folding the wool over until the piece you're working with is full; leave the bundles to dry so you can re-use them. When the bundles are dry, simply pull the wool apart, releasing all the bits of stripper. It's best to do this over a dustbin.

4 Repeat steps 1 and 2 until the frame is completely stripped. Wash it with bicarbonate of soda mixed with some warm water. When all the stripper is removed, rinse off the soda.

5 Let the frame dry and finish by sanding with fine-grade sandpaper.

Cleaning varnished chairs

YOU WILL NEED
- Raw linseed oil
- White spirits
- Empty jar
- Fine-grade wire wool
- Scissors
- Clean rag

If the chair just needs a clean, a simple mix of linseed oil and white spirit will remove any paint marks and generally brighten the colour of the wood. Do not use this mixture on untreated wood, as the oil will soak in and darken its appearance. It will also remove any wax finish.

1 Mix 5 per cent raw linseed oil and 95 per cent white spirits together in a jar. Close the lid and shake.

2 With the fine-grade wire wool, rub the mixture all over the frame in the direction of the grain.

3 Using a clean rag, wipe the frame. You will see the dirt lift onto the rag.

Stripping 2

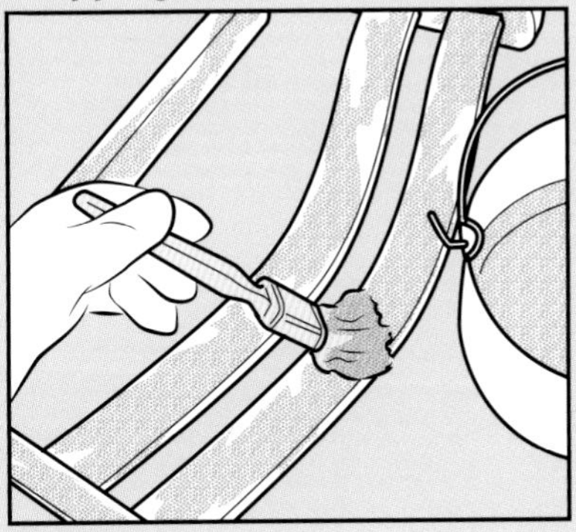

Stripping 3

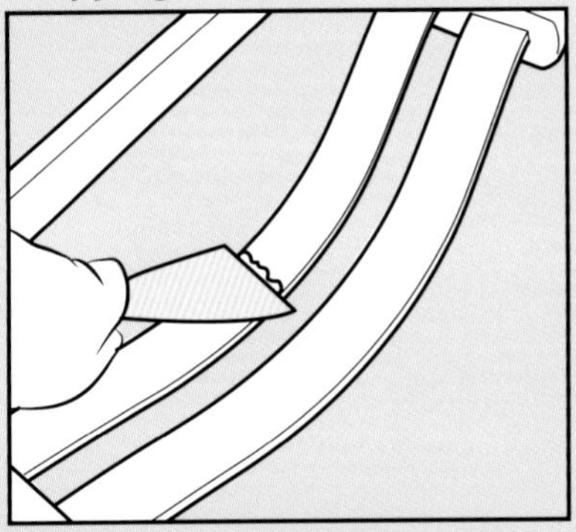

Stripping 4

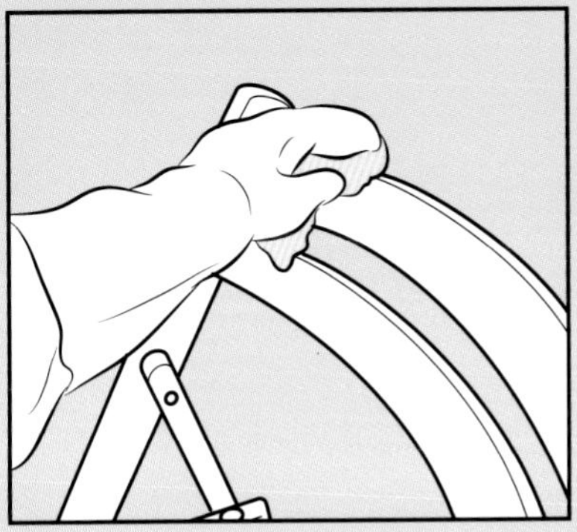

Cleaning 1

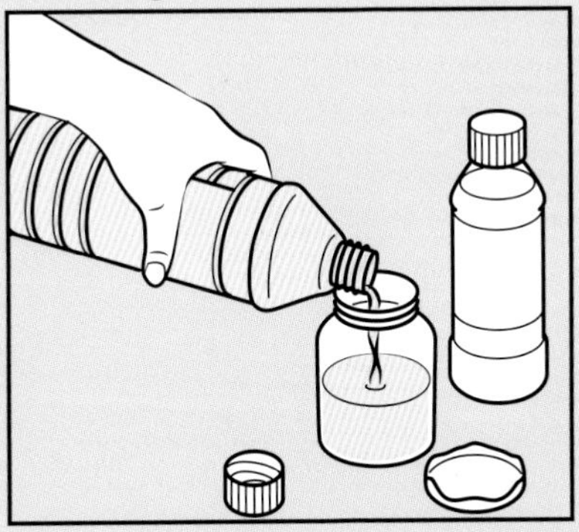

Cleaning 2

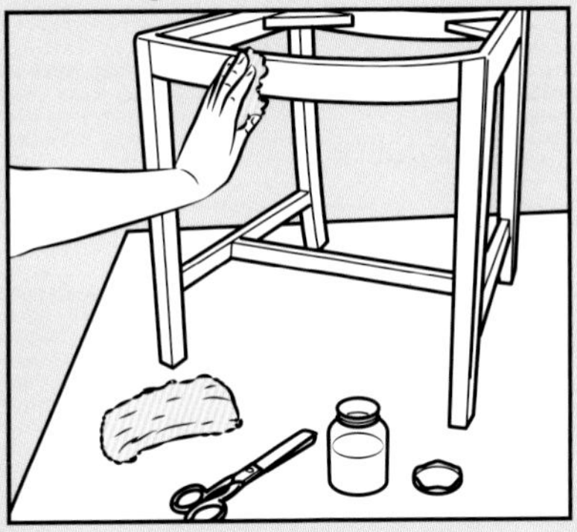

Cleaning 3

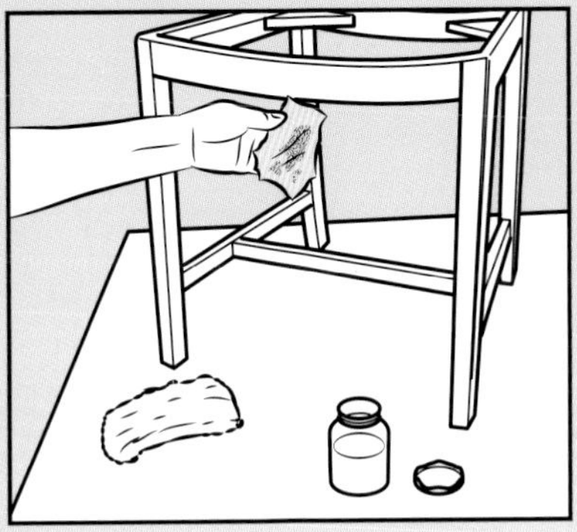

TIPS

Occasionally newly stripped wood shows patches of blue/black stains – similar to a bruise. This can be due to a fault that occurs during a sawmill process, but more often than not, it's simply a water stain. If you intend to keep the wood natural or finish with just a layer of wax, then you'll want to get rid of these marks. Oxalic acid is used for bleaching wood but is also an effective stain remover. When working with oxalic acid, take care to follow any instructions on the product and wear protective gloves and eyewear.

Wearing gloves, add 1 tablespoon of oxalic acid crystals to 100ml (½ cup) of tepid water in a jar – not the other way round – and stir. Leave for about 10 minutes. DO NOT use boiling or really hot water as the vapour is lethal. Follow any instructions on the oxalic acid container. Pre-soak the frame with warm water mixed with bicarbonate of soda. Whilst the wood is still damp, apply the acid evenly over the stain with a brush. When it is dry, thoroughly rinse the frame with water and a cloth. You might need to re-apply if the stain isn't removed. Be sure to always neutralise with water following treatment.

Frame maintenance

If your frame is falling apart, you'll need to strengthen it before upholstering. Many years of tacking and stapling might have made it look as if it's suffering from a bad case of woodworm. Or it might actually have woodworm, in which case you'll need to treat it quickly. On these pages you'll find a few common frame issues and their remedies.

Regluing & clamping loose joints

YOU WILL NEED
- PVA glue
- Damp cloth
- Ratchet tie-down clamp

Often the joints in a frame are pulling away from each other, leaving gaps and exposing dowels. If you don't fix this, your chair will be relying on just the upholstery to hold it together.

1 Make sure you can push the two pieces back into a firm position. If not, pull apart, sand them or do whatever is necessary to make them fit again. Fill the gap with PVA glue, keeping a damp cloth to hand to wipe up any spillages.

2 Clamp in place and leave overnight. Use the damp cloth to wipe away any seeping glue.

Reinforcing the seat with corner blocks

YOU WILL NEED
- Piece of card
- Compass
- Pencil
- Wood offcuts
  (good-quality pine or hardwood)
- Jigsaw
- Sandpaper
- Drill with countersink drill bit
- PVA glue
- Screws
- Screwdriver

When you are sure that your frame joints are firmly held together and there is no movement in the seat – but you'd still like it to be as strong as possible – then you can reinforce the corners with blocks of wood.

1 Make a template for the corner piece. To do this, hold a piece of card firmly against the straightest edge of the inside frame and as close to the leg as possible. Using a compass, scribe the cutting line. Hold the metal end of the compass against the inside of the frame with the pencil on the card. Run along the inside of the frame to the corner. What you are doing is making a copy of the curve of the frame onto the card.

2 Transfer this shape onto a wood offcut and, using a jigsaw, cut along the line. Bring it back to the frame to make sure the cut piece fits. You will probably need to sand or make a further cut to the straight-edged side of the block to get it to fit snugly. Once it fits, mark around the shape onto the frame. Repeat steps 1 and 2 for all the corners, making sure to name each piece so that you know where it goes.

3 Drill two holes into the long edge of the block, if possible using a countersink drill bit.

4 Squeeze some PVA glue onto the edges of the cut piece of wood, bring it back to the seat and line up with the marks.

5 Screw the corner block(s) in place.

Regluing & clamping 1

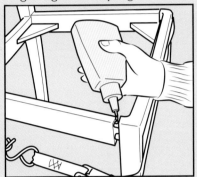

Reinforcing 1

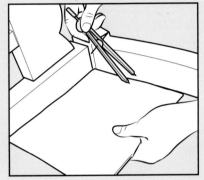

Reinforcing 4

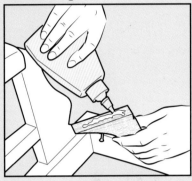

Regluing & clamping 2

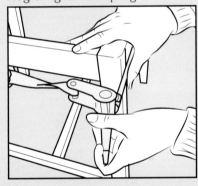

Reinforcing 2

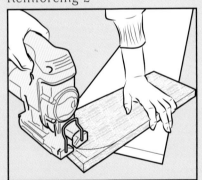

Reinforcing 5

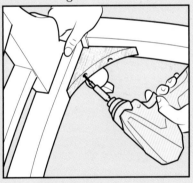

Reinforcing 3

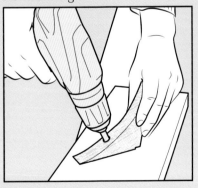

TIPS
If the seat will eventually be
sprung, you'll need to cut out a
curve on the longer edge of the
corner block so the springs can
get close to the frame.

Frame maintenance

Filling holes in frames

YOU WILL NEED
- PVA glue
- Fine sawdust
- Mixing vessel (to be thrown away afterwards)
- Small spatula
- Sandpaper

Years of upholstery can take its toll on a frame. Countless tack and staple holes could leave you with not much of a frame to upholster onto. The most effective (and also the cheapest) way to fill these holes is to use a simple mix of PVA glue and very fine sawdust. This filler is for use in non-visible areas, do not use it to fill any show wood damage.

1 Mix the PVA and sawdust together to make a paste.

2 Use a small spatula to fill the holes. Make sure you don't leave too much paste protruding, as you will only need to sand it down later.

3 Finish by sanding any rough edges.

Painting a wooden frame

Painting a frame is pretty easy and instantly gratifying. However, this is a change that's hard to reverse, so think carefully before proceeding. Check whether your piece is an antique; many prefer to be sympathetic to the history of the chair.

If you've already stripped the chair, go directly to step 3. If, however, you're looking at a chair with minimal damage but its last lick of paint still intact, you'll need to do a bit of prep first – start at step 1.

YOU WILL NEED
- Medium- and fine-grade sandpaper
- Tack cloth
- Paper and tape for protecting upholstery
- Dustsheet
- Facemask
- Spray primer
- Spray oil-based paint
- Small gloss roller
- Brush

1 Sand the chair all over in the direction of the grain using a medium-grade and then a fine-grade sandpaper. This will give the surface a 'key' for the paint to adhere to. Be wary of using a circular sander as this will leave circular marks in the frame if you press too hard. When you're finished, wipe off any dust with a tack cloth.

2 If you are only painting areas of show wood, then make sure any upholstery or stuffing that you don't want painted is protected with paper and tape. If you are applying a decorative effect such as a geometric pattern to the frame, use the tape to mark this out.

3 Lay a dustsheet down in a well-ventilated area away from any flying debris. Wearing a facemask, spray the chair with a wood primer. This will ensure that the final coat won't chip away and will also protect the wood itself. If you are spraying directly onto bare wood, you will need to use a primer. Hold the can about 18–20cm (7–8in) away from the chair and spray from top to bottom and side to side in short bursts for an even coverage. Make sure to start spraying off the frame. Continue onto the frame and stop spraying once away from the frame. Leave to dry between coats (you may need more than one). Finally, repeat this process with your top colour. Remember it's better to apply a few thin coats than one thick one, as thicker paint has a tendency to run.

4 If your chosen paint colour is unavailable as a spray, you can also use tinned paint. Use a gloss roller as much as possible and a paintbrush for hard-to-reach areas.

Filling 1

Filling 2

Painting 2

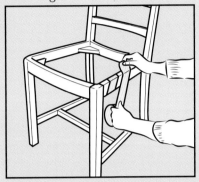

Painting 3

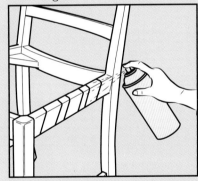

TIPS

Woodworm is the larvae of a wood-boring beetle. As the larvae matures, it bores its way out of the wood. Even if you suspect that the worm has long gone, it's still best to treat it. There are lots of treatments on the market – whichever you choose, be sure to follow the manufacturer's instructions.

Different paint colours need different undercoats, or primers. Generally, the darker the colour the darker the undercoat, but check the manufacturer's instructions before you paint.

Abrasives are graded by grit size. Lower numbers are coarse and higher numbers fine. It's unlikely you'll need to use anything coarser than 80 grit. 240 grit is very fine and perfect for preparing surfaces for finishing. Work your way through the grades starting with coarse, ending with fine.

Chairs can be delicate, so take care with anything power based. If your chair has intricate carving covered in paint and you want an even finish, use a sanding sponge, which can get into hard-to-reach places.

Kristin Jackson

Kristin defines herself as an interior designer and DIYer. She spent five years designing hotels all over the world at Design Continuum Inc. after graduating from the Art Institute of Atlanta in 2006. Needing a creative outlet after the birth of her daughter and her new role as a stay at home mum, she started writing her blog, *The Hunted Interior*. Her philosophy is to 'hunt' your home before buying new. In her words, 'Relocating a mirror, recovering a chair, painting a dresser are just a few easy things that can be done to give new life to an existing piece.'

FOR TUTORIALS
Painting a frame: page 100
Double piping: page 162
Corners: page 152

BEFORE   AFTER

Kristin discovered this chair on craigslist and snapped it up for $35. Thankfully, she wasn't put off by the burgundy and gold paint and the out-dated cover. She could see past all this and was drawn in by the beautiful lines of the chair, and managed to transform it in just one day.

I admire Kristin's bold use of fabrics on this piece – the beautiful Chiang Mai fabric on the back, mixed with the black-and-white ikat print – and the subtlety of using the brighter fabric on the out-of-sight part of the chair.

Kristin began by ripping the top cover from the chair; this was put to one side to be used as a template. The fillings were lifted and set aside to be re-used. As the chair is a reproduction, everything on the inside was fairly new.

She then had to remove the staples. I love staples because they are so much kinder to the wood, especially on a delicate frame, but removing them is another story. A pure blood, sweat and tears pursuit in some cases. As with many home upholsterers, you're not expected to be completely equipped for the job. You can however find a range of tools that are pretty standard in any toolbox and are perfectly adequate. Kristin used needle-nose pliers, a flat-head screwdriver and a pair of wire cutters to remove hard to budge staples.

Next, she prepared the frame for painting and, after a few rounds of sanding, priming and more sanding, she finished with a coat of Sherwin Williams ProClassic paint, chosen for its enamel-like finish.

Kristin sourced the Chiang Mai fabric by ripping apart a spare pillow. She cut the fabric from one of the templates, positioned it, pulled it taut and stapled it onto the back of the chair. The old fillings for the back were repositioned and covered in Seeing Spots ikat fabric from Waverly. For the seat, the old fillings were set in position and covered in more of the ikat fabric. Kristin worked the corners of the seat, stapled and trimmed back to the edge of the show wood. She asked a local upholsterer to make the double piping. She then hot glued it around the edges, covering up the staples.

Don't be afraid to lose control. Have fun with patterns, textures and colours

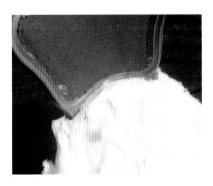

I asked Kristin what she learnt throughout the upholstering process, 'As this was my first upholstering attempt, I learned that you need to take the time to complete every step properly to achieve a professional look. If you mess up a staple (or twelve), don't just move on to the next one. Take the time to fix your mistakes before moving on to the next step. You will end up with a better result.'

CHAIR STYLE
A reproduction Bergere chair.

FABRIC USED
Chiang Mai from Schumacher and Seeing Spots in Noir from Waverly.

ORIGINAL STATE
Not bad condition. Just needed a refresh.

CHANGES MADE
Painted the frame, changed the fabrics and re-stapled.

TIME SPENT
One day.

Jude Dennis

Jude has spent over 15 years in the creative industries of film, theatre, fashion and events, making props, designing, dressing and painting sets. Enjoying the creative environment, but disillusioned by the temporary nature of the industry, Jude re-discovered her craft roots and began studying Traditional and Modern Upholstery at the London Metropolitan University. She creates chairs that are artistic, but also functional, blending traditional and modern techniques in her use of materials and fabrics. With her forward-thinking approach to upholstery design and her love of textiles, Jude has picked up many awards along the way.

FOR TUTORIALS
Tension springs: page 118
Traditional stuffing: page 124
Rubberised hair: page 128
Piped box cushion: page 80

BEFORE   AFTER

I like the two guises of this chair and the attention to detail given to both. From the handmade leather straps – a real show of patience and skill – to Jude's signature hand-stitched detail on the seat and back. The final look was an organic process, Jude taking inspiration from the chair itself. When the sheepskin arrived, it sat so perfectly in its uncut form that, rather than cutting the skin and covering the chair entirely, which was the original intention, Jude decided to leave it whole. The chair also looked great without the sheepskin, showing more of its original form. Instead of choosing just one look, Jude opted for both by making the sheepskin removable. The seat and back were covered in 100 per cent linen and Jude employed a traditional leather hand-stitching technique for the straps to secure the sheepskin.

Heidi, the American rocking chair, was a £5 eBay find. It was clear the chair had been through some tough times. Having removed the upholstery, Jude began work repairing the broken frame. The show wood was stripped and re-polished, returning it to its natural state.

To me the chair doesn't need to have a designer name or iconic status to be interesting, having character and potential interests me more

A mixture of traditional and modern materials and techniques were employed for the upholstery. The back and seat were sprung with close-coil springs. The springs in the back were covered with hessian and a lumber and head rest formed with some coir. A layer of rubberised hair was stapled over this and given further shape and stability with some stuffing ties. A layer of cotton felt and polyester wadding were then added before the top cover.

Jude removed the wings and upholstered them separately, creating their shape with foam. The chair now looks less top heavy and the reduction in buttons from four to three has given a more balanced feel. The seat was also given a new foam interior and both the seat and back were finished with Jude's hand-stitching detail in matching linen thread. The handmade leather straps and buckles were then attached to the bottom, back and sides of the chair, ensuring a snug fit for the sheepskin.

CHAIR STYLE
Heidi American rocking chair.

FABRIC USED
Gotland sheepskin from the Organic Tannery in Herefordshire and 100 per cent linen fabric for the seat and back. Finished with matching linen thread.

ORIGINAL STATE
Broken frame. Worn out and sagging upholstery.

CHANGES MADE
The broken frame was fixed and the show wood restored. Complete reupholstery.

TIME SPENT
The total time was around two weeks, almost half of which was taken up with learning how to stitch the buckles.

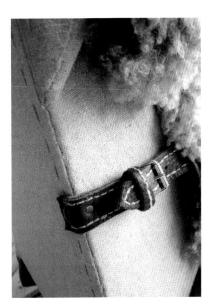

The bare bones

Seeing a chair 'naked' for the first time can be quite a traumatic experience and it may be difficult to visualise it covered in fabric. So, it's good to know beforehand what goes where and the general processes involved, allowing you to think ahead without being intimidated.

ORDER OF WORK

As a general rule, you should start with rebuilding the insides, followed by the outsides. The following is an outline of the process of rebuilding a standard handmade chair; if your chair is machine-built, for instance, the process may differ slightly.

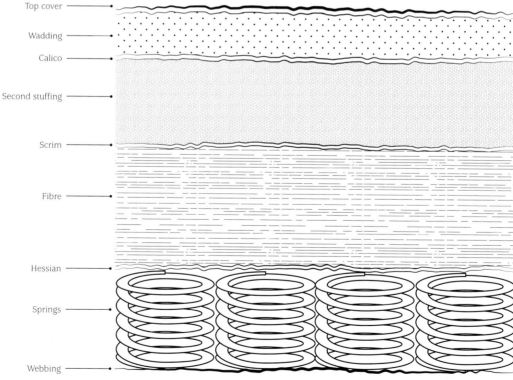

Top cover	
Wadding	
Calico	
Second stuffing	
Scrim	
Fibre	
Hessian	
Springs	
Webbing	

Diagram showing the order of materials for traditional upholstery.

FIRST FIXING

Insides:
1. Upholster the arms and wings.
2. Upholster the back.
3. Upholster the seat.

The arms and back need to be completed to the top cover, but left temporary tacked on the outside of the arm and back stuffing rails. Working in this order is not absolutely necessary, but it will make accessing tuckaways and cutting much simpler.

SECOND FIXING

1. Permanently attach the seat top cover to the top of the side and back stretcher rails, and bring under the front stretcher rail.
2. Bring the cover down from the arms and back and staple over the seat fabric.
3. Apply any piping and borders.

THIRD FIXING

1. Pad the outside arms and cover.
2. Pad and cover the outside back.
3. Finish with any trimmings or nails.
4. Attach some bottom cloth.

SHAPE

Always think ahead to what you want to achieve. Do some research, make some sketches and look in shops and online. Think about how big your chair should be. If the frame is delicate and the seat is small, then take a refined approach with the stuffing – be sympathetic to its size. You want it to be even and not lumpy, but you also want it to be strong enough to take your weight.

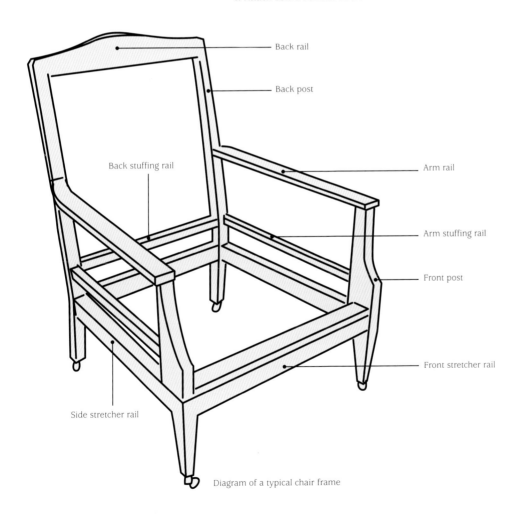

Back rail

Back post

Back stuffing rail

Arm rail

Arm stuffing rail

Front post

Front stretcher rail

Side stretcher rail

Diagram of a typical chair frame

Webbing a seat

You're likely to encounter many different kinds of webbing; most variations are due to the age of the furniture and its country of origin. In the USA and Europe, webbing tends to be positioned closely together, almost touching, and is plain woven. In the UK, there are gaps left between the webs and more often than not they are twill woven, giving a herringbone effect. As well as jute-based webbings, flexible webbings are often used in modern furniture.

YOU WILL NEED
- High-quality webbing
- Tailor's chalk
- G-clamp
- Staple gun
- Staples
- Tacks
- Hammer
- Web strainer
- Scissors

TIPS
Chair backs and arms will also need to be webbed. Remember that these areas don't need to support as much weight as the seat and are more to keep the shape. For the arms, the amount of webbing you use will depend on the space between the bottom rail and the top and the distance between the sides. The back will need more webbing than the arms as it will need to give more support. If you are fixing springs, you will need to web in the same way as you would a seat.

Regardless of the chair's origins, the webbing on any seat is a crucial support element. It must take the weight of the layers of stuffing, linings, springs and of course the person sitting on it. With this in mind, use the best webbing you can afford and strong fixings.

For a drop-in seat with minimal stuffing, it's best to web no more than a web-space apart and on the upper side of the seat. If the chair is to be sprung, position the webs closer together and on the underside of the seat. Use large tacks (at least 13mm/½in) or 14mm (½in) staples.

1 Work out an even positioning of webbing, marking the frame with tailor's chalk as a guide. If you are webbing a drop-in seat, clamp the frame to a sturdy table.

2 Keeping the webbing on the roll, fold back the end, and staple or tack it in place. Staple in three rows of three, or tack in the 'W' formation. There are more layers to follow that will also need to be fixed to the frame, so with this in mind, keep the webbing away from the edge.

3 Feed the webbing through the hole in the front of the web strainer, out the back, and secure with the pin. Pull the webbing tight to hold the pin in place.

4 Position the lip of the strainer on the frame and pull it towards you and down. Make sure the webbing is very tight. However, if you hear creaking wood noises, then you have strained too far. Take care when webbing a drop-in seat, as these lack the support of the chair frame and can easily distort.

5 While holding the strainer, staple the web or tack in a triangle shape.

6 Release the strainer, cut the webbing, fold over and fix again in a reverse triangle if you are using tacks.

7 Continue to web in one direction. When you've finished, web in the opposite direction, weaving each web over and under. Alternate the weave with each web. Remember to weave the webbing through your completed webs before stapling.

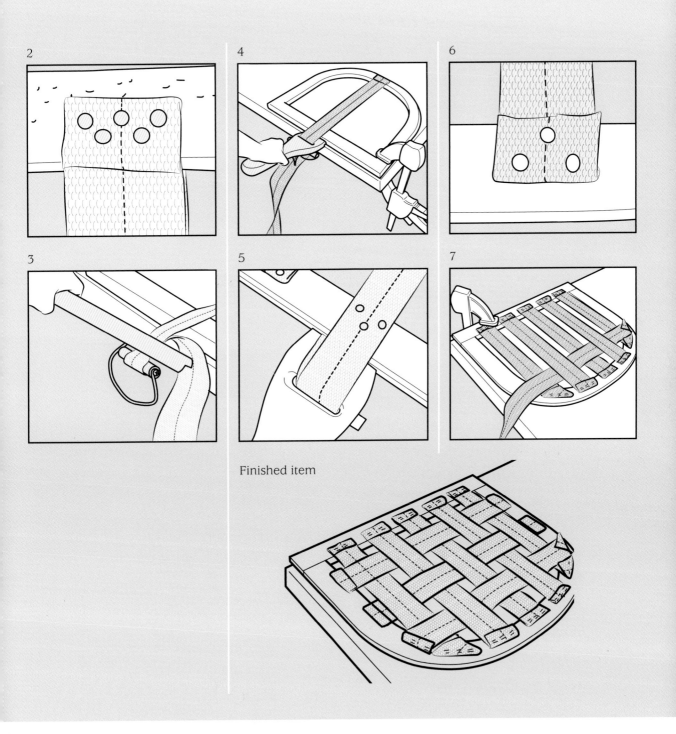

Finished item

Knots, ties & stitches

The following knots, ties and stitches must be mastered in order to upholster a chair using a traditional technique. They are used to control loose fillings, position springs or for holding fabrics together discreetly.

Slip knot

YOU WILL NEED
- Nylon thread, 4 cord or slipping thread
- Suitable needle

One of the most commonly used knots in upholstery, the slip knot is the starting point for most ties and stitches. It can be loosened easily, making it great for positioning and repositioning buttons.

1 Thread the needle. Pass the thread into the fabric and back out towards you.

2 Unthread the needle.

3 Holding both threads with your fingers, take the shorter length over the top of the longer length.

4 Continue to take the shorter thread under both held threads and bring through the loop.

5 Repeat step 4.

6 Pull the longer length of thread to tighten.

Bridle ties

YOU WILL NEED
- Tailor's chalk
- Nylon thread or 4 cord
- Spring needle

Bridle ties are used to help position loose stuffing and keep it in place. The pattern of the ties should follow the shape of the frame edge and make for an even coverage of stuffing.

1 Mark out the positioning of the ties with tailor's chalk. Follow the shape of the frame to make the ties evenly spaced. Thread the spring needle and make a slip knot. For this drop-in seat I'm making the knot about 2.5cm (1in) in from the frame on the upper side of the seat.

2 Thread the cord through the hessian and come back on yourself by about 1.5–2.5cm (½–1in) and back up through the hessian. This backstitching will prevent any gaps from appearing in the stuffing.

3 Continue making these loops around your frame. The loops should just fit your hand. Finish with a knot.

Slip knot 1

Slip knot 4

Bridle ties 1

Slip knot 2

Slip knot 5

Bridle ties 2

Slip knot 3

Slip knot 6

Bridle ties 3

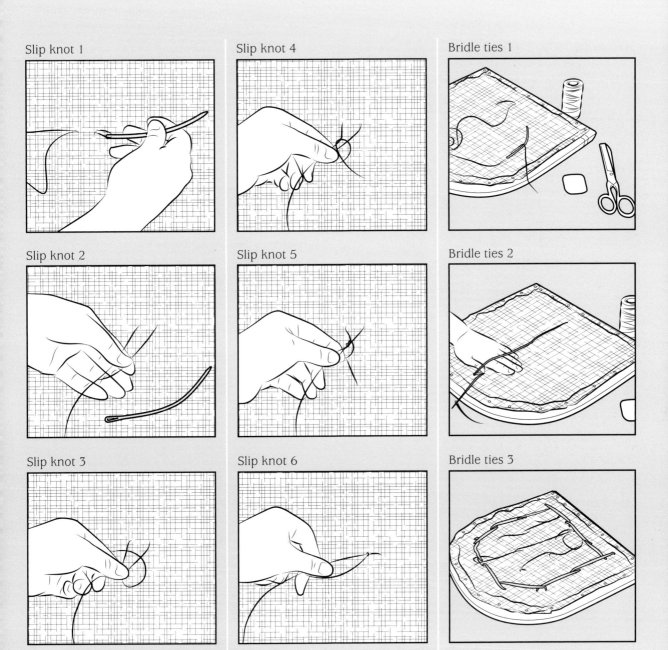

Knots, ties & stitches

Stuffing ties

YOU WILL NEED
- Tailor's chalk
- Nylon thread or 4 cord
- Bayonet needle

Stuffing ties hold your hessian- or scrim-covered stuffing in place. As with bridle ties, the positioning needs to be even.

1 Mark out the positioning of the ties with tailor's chalk. Follow the shape of the frame and make sure the ties are evenly spaced.

2 Thread a bayonet needle and make a slip knot. Pass the needle down through the stuffing, out of the webbed base, and back up so that the slip knot sits on the top of the seat. Note: if your seat is sprung, stop the needle when it passes through the hessian that sits on top of the springs. Do not pass through the springs to the webbed base.

3 Work your way around the seat with running stitches about a hand's width apart. Move 2.5–5cm (1–2in) forwards on the underside before returning the needle to the top.

4 When returning the needle to the top, pull on the cord while patting the previous stitch down. This will tighten the stitching and pull the layers together. When you are sure the seat is even, finish off with a simple knot.

Clove hitch knot

YOU WILL NEED
- Laid cord

The clove-hitch knot is used primarily for lashing springs with laid cord.

1 Bring the cord over and under the spring edge.

2 Pass this end over the cord and over the spring edge.

3 Bring the cord back up through the loop.

Blind stitch

YOU WILL NEED
- Glove (preferably fingerless)
- Nylon thread or 4 cord
- Bayonet needle
- Tailor's chalk

A blind stitch is used to control and shape loose stuffing. Two rows of blind stitch can be used if a high edge is required. The first row of blind stitching should be positioned just above the tacks or staples on the front of the chair frame. Position the next row of blind stitching about 2.5cm (1in) above the first. As you stitch, regulate the stuffing to keep the shape of the chair even. If you are left-handed, follow the instructions for this stitch and top stitch (following) in reverse – working from right to left. Blind stitch is similar to top stitch but you should not see the stitches on top of the seat. The loops of thread remain hidden inside, controlling the stuffing.

1 Wear a glove for this process, as it is really hard on the hands. Thread a bayonet needle and pass it into the seat at an upwards angle so that the needle appears out of the top. Return the needle to the start position without leaving the top of the seat. Make a slip knot.

2 Move to the right by about 2.5cm (1in) and again pass the needle through the covered stuffing with the threaded eye closest to you. Stop before you see the thread appearing on the top of the seat and return the needle back through the stuffing at about a 45-degree angle. You can mark the intervals using tailor's chalk to ensure your stitches are even.

3 Before the needle is all the way out, wrap the thread from the left-hand side three times around the needle. Continue to bring the needle out of the stuffing. Pull the cord sharply to the right.

4 Continue this process along the seat.

Stuffing ties

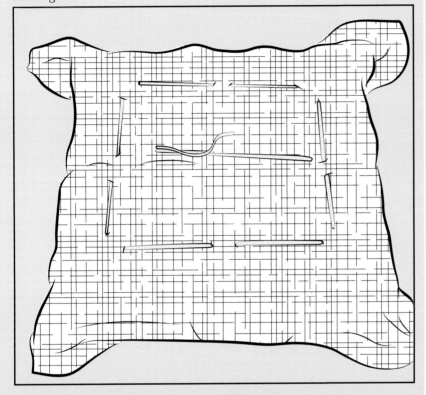

Blind stitch 2

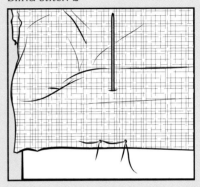

Blind stitch 3

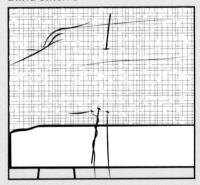

Clove hitch knot

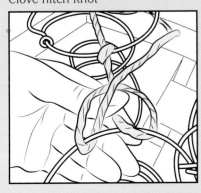

Blind stitch 1

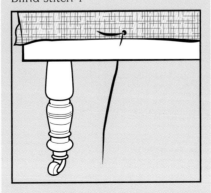

Blind stitch 4

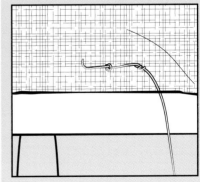

Knots, ties & stitches

Top stitch

YOU WILL NEED
- Glove (preferably fingerless)
- Nylon thread or 4 cord
- Bayonet needle
- Tailor's chalk
- Regulator

The top stitch is essentially a repeat of the blind stitch, but with one difference. The needle is brought completely out of the top of the seat and returned, rather than stopping short of the top. Its purpose is to shape the top edge of the seat.

1 Regulate the stuffing so that it is even along the front top edge of the seat. Wear a glove for this process, as it is really hard on the hands. As with the blind stitch, thread the needle and start with a slip knot on the seat facing.

2 Move to the right by about 2.5cm (1in); you can mark this distance on the hessian with tailor's chalk. Pass the needle through the hessian-covered stuffing with the eye closest to you. Bring the needle out of the top of the seat, move back to your first stitch and return the needle back through the stuffing.

3 Before the needle is all the way out, wrap the thread from the left-hand side three times around the needle. Pull the needle completely out.

4 Pull the cord sharply to the right so that the knot is tight and the roll is starting to form. Be sure to regulate the stuffing so that your shape is even.

Slip stitch

YOU WILL NEED
- Small curved needle
- Slipping thread

The slip stitch is used mainly in the finishing stages of upholstery. It's a strong stitch that holds fabrics together. This example shows stitching an outside back to an inside back.

1 With a small curved needle and some slipping thread, make a slip knot. Position the knot where it can eventually be hidden, under some piping for example. Pass the needle through the piping from the outside back to the inside back.

2 With the needle facing down, go into the fabric as close to the piping as possible for about 1.5cm (½in) and out again.

3 Pass the needle back through the piping from the outside back to the inside back.

4 Continue this process, pulling gently as you go to tighten the thread. Finish with a simple knot.

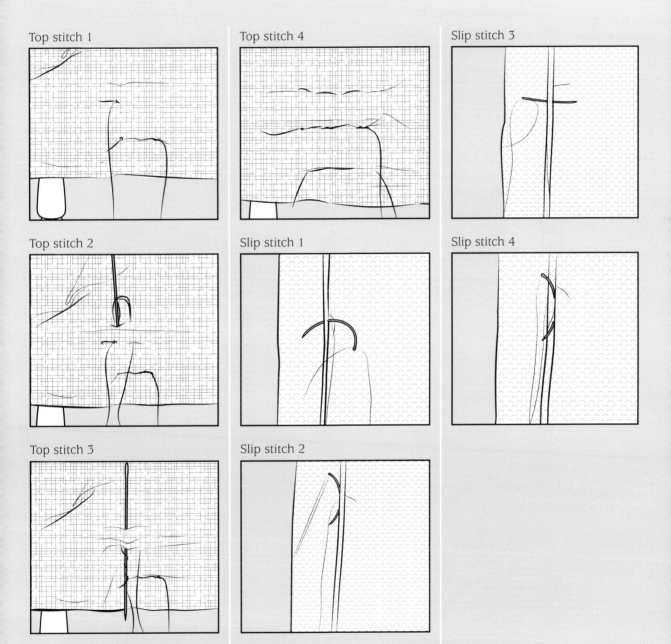

Top stitch 1

Top stitch 4

Slip stitch 3

Top stitch 2

Slip stitch 1

Slip stitch 4

Top stitch 3

Slip stitch 2

Types of springs

There are so many styles of chairs, sofas and chaises, both traditional and modern – all with their individual needs and quirks. One thing they all have in common, though, is that someone will sit on them, and that person needs to be comfortable. Comfort is partly achieved by the use of springs. Usually the type of spring or spring system depends on the size of the chair and whether it is a modern or traditional piece.

Of course, when you ripped down your chair you made detailed notes. You paid careful attention to the upholstery, how it was attached and in what order. Now you need to pay the same level of attention to the springs. Opening a chair up to be faced with a blur of twine and coiled metal can be quite alarming. However, don't be overwhelmed. Yes, it takes years of experience to lash a Chesterfield in half an hour. But more important is common sense and hard work, even if it takes you a long time to achieve the perfect end result.

If the springs are in a good condition, re-use them. As a general rule, springs should stand up straight when under no tension, should compress easily and not be covered in rust. The following are a few commonly found suspension systems.

Compression springs

SPRING UNITS
A relatively modern development in the spring world is the spring unit (below). As the name suggests, a number of springs are linked and held together to form a single unit. You can buy standard sizes or have a bespoke one made for your chair – with obvious price differences. All you have to do is secure the unit to the frame and cover it with hessian. Some units contain springs encased in calico.

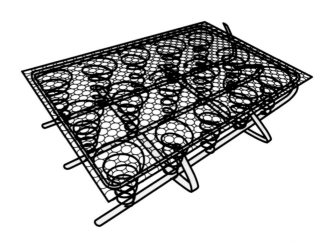

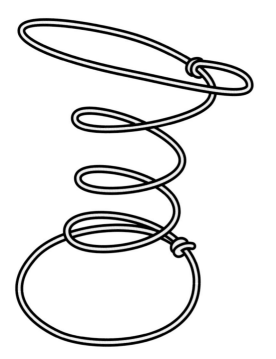

DOUBLE CONE SPRINGS
Double cone springs (left) come in a range of heights (10–30cm/4–12in) and gauges (thicknesses), from 8swg to 22swg (swg stands for 'standard wire gauge').

The lower the swg, the thicker the spring and the firmer it will feel. So, 8-gauge is very firm and 22-gauge is very soft. In the seat, 8–10-gauge tend to be used with the softer ones being more commonly used for chair backs and arms.

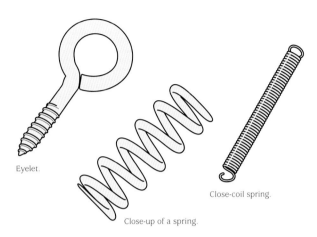

Eyelet.

Close-up of a spring.

Close-coil spring.

Tension springs

CLOSE-COIL SPRINGS

Close-coil springs are stretched across the width of a chair back or seat and attach to the side rails. As with traditional coil springs, the firmer ones are used in the seat and the softer ones in the back. The springs are spaced around 5.5–6.5cm (2–2½in) apart and can be attached using various methods; usually a metal eye is screwed into the frame or a metal plate is attached to the top of the frame. If the springs might be exposed, for example under a removable cushion, they need to be covered.

SERPENTINE SPRINGS

Serpentine, no-snag or zigzag springs come on a roll ready to be cut to size. If you don't have a workbench cutter or heavy-duty bolt cutters, it's best to get the springs cut professionally. The springs are held in place with clips that attach to the top of the frame with nails. The springs come in varying gauges, measured in the same way as the double-cone springs.

Traditional double cone springs

SELECTING

Do you want your seat to be hard or soft? It's all about personal choice. If you like quite a solid base, try 9-gauge. For a slightly softer effect, choose 10-gauge.

POSITIONING

The goal is to have an even feel and to achieve this, the springs will have an even look. Most of your weight will hit the centre of the chair, so make sure there isn't a big open space right there. Position the springs no more than 5cm (2in) apart. You don't want any gaping holes between them.

LASHING

Think ahead to the lashing (the term used for tying springs together and to the frame with twine). You'll lash the springs in straight lines front to back and from side to side, and in some cases across the diagonal. When everything is lashed you'll need to cover it with hessian. With both these things in mind, turn the springs so that the knots or open ends are facing inwards. You want anything sharp away from the twines or the hessian, which will be pulled taut around the edges.

Note that if you're springing the back of a chair, the same rules apply as for the seat.

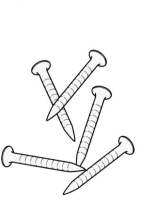

Serpentine nails.

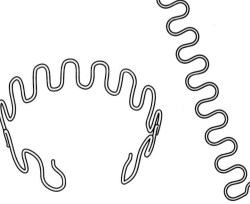

Serpentine springs.

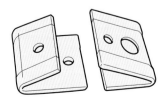

Clips.

Using springs

Attaching springs to webbing

YOU WILL NEED
- Springs
- Tailor's chalk or marker pen
- Nylon thread
- Scissors
- Spring needle or large curved needle

1 Position the springs on the webbing with the spring knots or open ends facing inwards and draw around them using chalk or a marker.

2 Each spring will need to be held in place by three or four knots. Cut a long piece of nylon thread. Thread the spring needle and push from underneath the seat through the webbing right next to the spring.

3 Loop up, over and back down through the webbing. Fix with a slip knot.

4 In three or four equally spaced parts of the spring, loop the nylon from below up, over and back down through the webbing and knot. Make sure that every loop and knot is very tight – you shouldn't be able to turn the spring. Repeat this process for all of the springs. There's no need to start from scratch for each one; if your thread is long enough you can connect them all. Finish with a double knot.

TYPICAL SPRING POSITIONS

Attaching 1

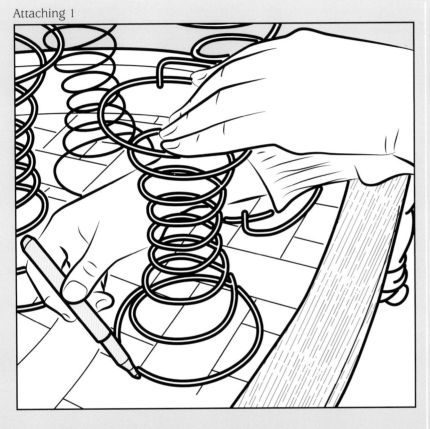

Attaching 2

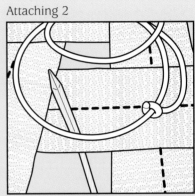

Attaching 3

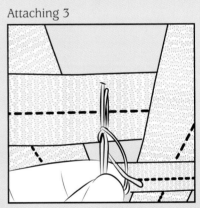

Attaching 4

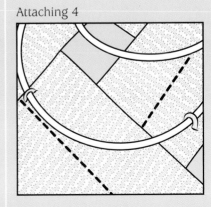

Using springs

Close-coil springs

YOU WILL NEED
- Ruler
- Pencil
- Metal eyelets
- Close-coil springs
- Strong wire cutters
- Flat-head screwdriver

1 Mark the spring spacing on your frame. This is generally around 5–6.5cm (2–3in). Screw metal eyelets into the inside of the frame on opposite sides.

2 Ask your spring supplier for the correct stretch for the spring. Generally it's about 2.5cm (1in). Measure the distance between the eyelets, minus 2.5cm (1in) and cut your coil to this length using wire cutters. Fold out the end of the hook (take this into account when measuring). This can be tricky; use a flat-head screwdriver and brute force.

3 Hook one end of the coil into the eyelet, stretch across the gap, and hook into the opposite eyelet.

Serpentine springs

YOU WILL NEED
- Serpentine springs
- Ruler
- Pencil
- Clips
- Nails
- Hammer
- Laid cord

If you don't have a bench-mounted wire cutter, it's best to have your springs cut by a professional. If you are removing any springs, take one along to show the size. The way to measure a spring is to flatten it underfoot next to a ruler or just count the curves.

1 The springs should have a shallow arch – think about the overall height you want and the layers that need to follow. Work out the positioning of your springs. They should be about 10–12.5cm (4–5in) apart. Mark this on your frame.

2 Position and nail down the clip on the inside edge of the rail with the folded side facing inward. Repeat on the opposite edge of the frame.

3 Make sure that your springs have a kink in both ends; this will keep them from sliding out of the clip. Loop one end of the spring into the clip. Working from the opposite side of the frame, pull the spring towards you and place in the clip.

4 Nail down the open part of the clip.

5 To keep the springs from moving from side to side, either lash them (see page 122) or use ready-made clips, which simply attach between springs. Cut some laid cord long enough to run from one edge of your frame to the other and half again. Tie a clove hitch knot to the middle of the first spring. Bring the cord to the next spring and tie another knot. Make sure the cord is taut but not pulling the springs together.

6 Hammer two tacks onto both sides of the frame. Loop the loose cord around the tacks and hammer home.

Close-coil springs 1

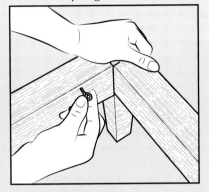

Close-coil springs 2

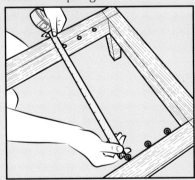

Close-coil springs 3

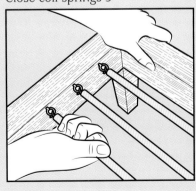

Serpentine springs 2

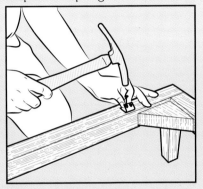

Serpentine springs 3

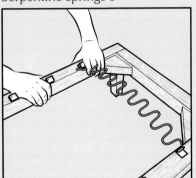

Serpentine springs 4

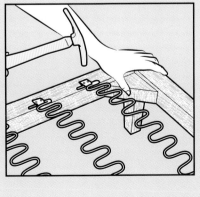

Serpentine springs 5

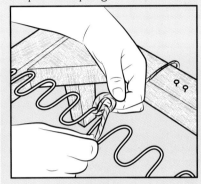

Serpentine springs 6

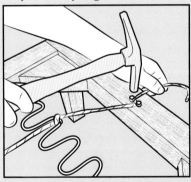

Serpentine springs: finished item

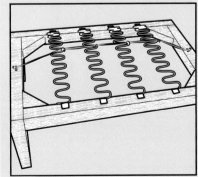

Lashing the springs

Lashing will require a little thinking time before you dive in and start knotting. You may also find yourself tying and re-tying a few times until you're completely happy.

YOU WILL NEED

- Laid cord
- Tape measure
- Scissors
- 16mm improved tacks
- Hammer

- Hessian
- Staple gun (optional)
- Staples (optional)
- Spring needle
- Nylon thread

TIPS
When lashing, look at what you are doing from all angles. Make sure everything is balanced and symmetrical.

Remember that the purpose of lashing is to control the movement of the springs. They should only move up and down; however, you want to make a slightly curved overall shape with the springs. In order to do this, the springs that sit centrally need to be upright while the outer springs should lean slightly towards the edge of the frame. As you compress the springs with your hand, they should return to their upright position. If your springs are tall, they will need some central lashing to hold and keep the middle of the spring in position.

1 Measure and cut a length of laid cord that reaches twice across the springs. This will give you enough cord for knots and pulling.

2 Hammer a 16mm improved tack onto the frame in line with the centre of the springs, but don't hammer it completely in. Hammer two more tacks in the same way on the opposite frame edge. Make a clove hitch knot onto the edge of the first spring (see page 112). Compress the spring nearest the frame and tie the cord around the tack, but do not hammer the tack home. You may need to secure with another tack.

3 Make another clove hitch knot on the opposite side of the spring. Continue the cord to the next spring. Make sure the gap between the two springs is the same at the top as it is at the base. Continue this process until you reach the opposite side.

4 Take one end of cord and wrap it around the remaining tack, compressing the spring with your free hand. This can be quite strenuous, but use the tack as a lever to help you bring the spring down. The end result should be that the centre springs stand upright and the side springs face slightly outwards.

5 Lash all the springs in this way from left to right and from front to back, and over the diagonal if necessary. Keep in mind the eventual goal: to have the springs held together in a unit, unable to move from side to side or knock into each other. Check from all sides that everything is even and, when you're happy with the lashing, hammer in the tacks to secure.

6 Cover your springs in 12oz hessian (or heavier). Measure, cut and position the hessian over the springs, remembering to keep the threads running from left to right and from back to front. Keep the edge of the hessian away from the edge of the frame – there are more layers to come. Turn over the edge and staple or tack it. Pull taut over the springs to the opposite side and staple. Repeat on the remaining sides. When evenly positioned and tight, continue to staple or tack until all the edges are held down.

7 With your spring needle and nylon thread, tie the hessian to the springs in exactly the same way as for steps 2 and 3 in 'Attaching springs to webbing' on page 118. Your seat is now ready for stuffing.

1

4

7

2

5

3

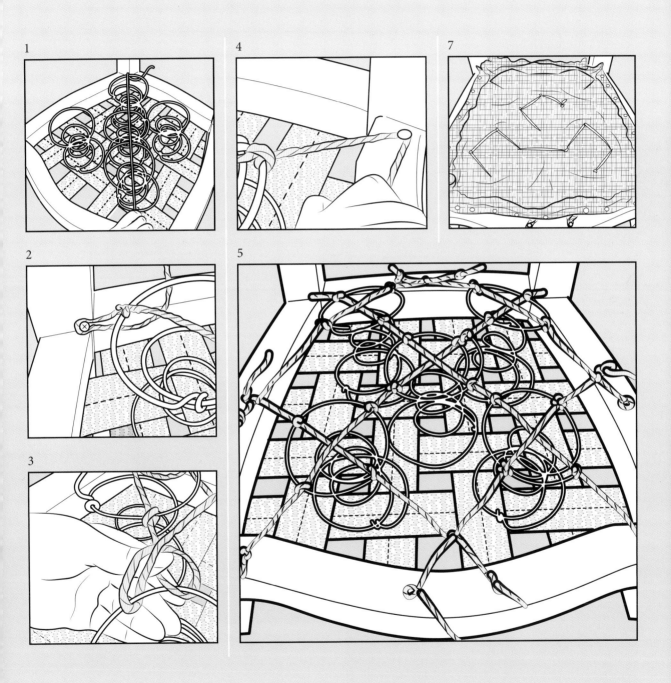

Stuffing

There are many ways to stuff a chair, and no doubt you'll encounter a few with each one you uncover. Replacing like for like would seem a good way to go, but if you're faced with traditional hand stitching, it's obviously trickier than some of the modern equivalents. Developments in materials have made the upholstery process easier and faster, so use whatever material works best for you.

Trying to describe every style of chair and how to stuff each one would be a mammoth task. With every chair you uncover, you'll find there is more to learn. Whatever materials you decide to use, the outcome should be the same: to make the chair look great and be comfortable to sit in. Think about the shapes you are creating and the size of the piece. Having to squeeze yourself into a chair is never good! Here are some of the more common materials and methods.

SEATS

- The highest point on the seat should be just forwards of centre – you should slide to the back of the chair, not forwards.
- Generally, you want a solid, firm edge; this can be created with any sort of stuffing.
- Any type of stuffing you use needs to be securely tied or glued in place.
- A slight overhang on the seat gives the impression that the seat is more upright than it actually is.

ARMS

Arms need to be identical. Stand back from the chair occasionally and have a proper look. Double-check with a tape measure.

PREPARING THE FRAME

If your chair was traditionally stuffed before then it likely has a bevelled edge on the front of the chair. If not, make one using a rasp. The area that is bevelled should be the same width as the top of a 13mm (½in) tack and should be at a 45-degree angle to the front of the frame.

Left: 1940s Utility chair upholstered by Hannah Stanton.
Above: Uncovering the original stuffing in Marianne Songbird's chair.
Right: Armchair by Gubi.

Traditional stuffing

It is the norm to have two stuffings and linings: the first to form the underlying shapes, and the second to soften up the chair and bring back the comfort. This example uses black fibre for the first stuffing. It's a pretty dense material, so it holds its shape well. Bridle and stuffing ties secure it. The blind and top stitch manipulate the fibre to create that desirable firm edge. Hair and cotton linter felt create the second, softer stuffing.

First stuffing

YOU WILL NEED
- Hessian
- Nylon thread
- Bayonet needle
- Curved needle
- Black fibre
- Tape measure
- Scrim
- Scissors
- Tacks
- Hammer
- Chalk
- Calico
- Regulator
- Leather gloves
- Hair
- Cotton wadding
- Cotton felt

1 Make bridle ties in the hessian (see page 110) with the nylon thread and curved needle. Position them so they are evenly spaced and follow the shape of the seat, back or arm.

2 Tease the fibre to remove any lumps, cup it in your hand and roll it under the bridle ties. This action can cause the lumps to return, so continue to tease the fibre with your fingers throughout this process. The fibre needs to be a touch denser towards the front of the seat.

3 Measure the seat front to back and from side to side Add approximately 5cm (2in) to each edge and cut some scrim – it's more flexible than hessian and can be shaped easily. Position the scrim over the fibre so the threads run from side to side and from front to back. It's really important to keep it straight. Tack one side, then the opposite side, then the remaining two sides.

4 Now add some stuffing ties to hold all that fibre in place. Measure in from the edge by about 10cm (4in) and mark all around with chalk; also mark the bridle tie positioning.

5 Bring the needle down through the stuffing and stop when you hear it come through the hessian beneath. Don't continue through the springs and webbing.

6 Pull up each tie and pat down the previous one to tighten it up.

7 You now need to add more fibre to create a firm edge. Don't forget the sides between the seat and the arms – you don't want this area to be hollow. If you find it hard to judge, lay some scrap calico over the fibre, temporary tack in place and sit on it. Run your hands down the sides to check the fullness, then remove the calico. For the firm front edge, tease a large amount of fibre and shape it like a sausage. Take out the temporary tacks, lift up the edge of the scrim and stuff the sausage along the front. You'll probably be surprised by how much fibre you can fit in. Keep in mind the slight overhang you are hoping to achieve.

8 Now fold and tuck the scrim under the fibre so that you are temporary tacking through two pieces of scrim. This keeps the edges strong and the scrim is less likely to ravel. Check that the stuffing is even. If not, use a regulator to move the fibre into any hollow areas.

9 Permanently tack down onto the bevelled edge. You need to keep the scrim tight and the fibre solid. It's quite likely that your hands will hurt during this process, so wear leather gloves. Stand back to check the evenness, looking at the threads in the scrim. Are the threads in the same position on the left as they are on the right? The seat shown here has a slight forwards curve. Because of this the thread lines also curve. The line of pins indicate this curve.

10 Check how regular your stuffing is. If it is lumpy or there is more fibre on one side, use the regulator to move the fibre around. Put your regulator into the stuffing. Move your hand and the end of the regulator to the left or right. This will move the tip of the regulator to the left or right moving the fibre with it.

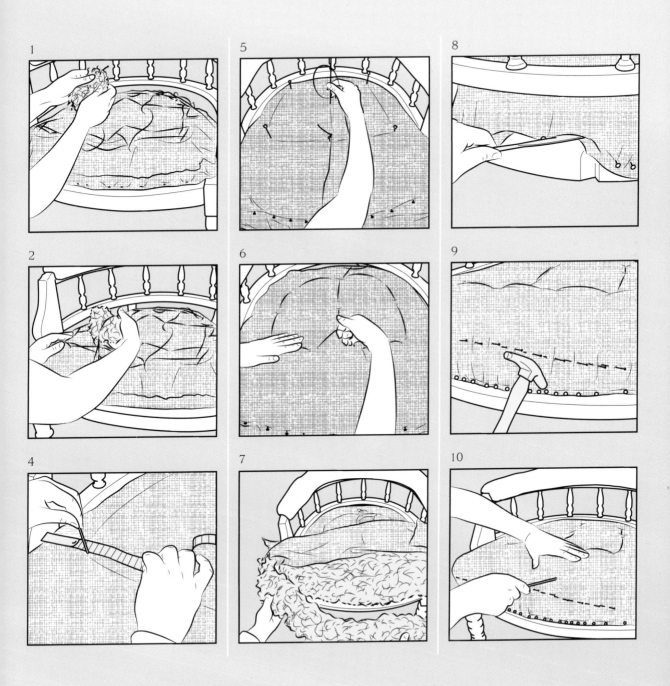

Traditional stuffing

11 Blind and top stitching is a slightly more relaxing, but possibly painful stage. The blind stitch holds the fibre in place and pulls it tightly to the front of the seat. This seat is to be quite high, so there are two rows of blind stitches. Start just above the seat rail where the scrim meets the frame. Mark 2.5cm (1in) spacings onto the frame with chalk.

12 For the blind stitch: begin with a slip knot on the left-hand side of the seat, just above the tacks. Start on the right if you are left-handed.

13 At every chalk mark, push your needle in through the front and out the top without bringing the thread completely through. Angle the needle and bring it back out through the front just to the left of where you entered. Wrap the twine three times around the needle, pull completely out and snap tightly to the right – after a couple of stitches you'll realise why you need your gloves!

14 Regulate the stuffing again, bringing more towards the front top edge, and continue to regulate throughout. For the top stitch: make a slip knot and start each stitch at every chalk mark. Constantly check from all angles that the line is even. You might want to draw a line along the top with chalk. Keep checking that you have that slight overhang.

Second stuffing

YOU WILL NEED
- Curved needle
- Nylon thread
- Tape measure
- Scissors
- Tacks
- Hammer
- Chalk
- Calico
- Regulator
- Leather gloves
- Hair
- Cotton felt

1 Make some bridle ties in the scrim with a curved needle and some nylon thread (see page 110). Tease the hair, then cup and roll it under the ties. Keep checking that there are no hollow areas and tease as you go.

2 Lay a piece of cotton felt over the hair, pushing it under the rails between the seat and the arm. With your hand, trim away any excess at the front.

3 Measure and cut some calico and temporary tack over the seat. It's good at this point to sit on the chair, or even to leave something heavy on it overnight.

4 Tear some cotton felt to cover the front of the seat. Lift up the calico at the front and position the felt over the stitch work. When you're happy with the positioning, make your cuts and permanently tack in place.

COTTON LINTER FELT
Cotton linter felt is beautifully soft. It comes in various thicknesses and can be used whole-thickness or halved, depending on the job at hand. It is used over traditional stuffing or rubberised hair. As with skin wadding, the cotton material keeps any hair from working its way through the calico and top fabric. You tear it rather than cut it, and feathering the edges can help with shaping.

With this drop-in seat, some pieces of felt were positioned over the dips made by the stuffing ties, then covered in a half-thickness layer of felt and finished with calico.

SKIN WADDING
As with poly wadding, skin wadding is used as the final soft lining before the top cover. The 'skin' keeps any stray hairs or fibres from protruding. It comes in quite short widths and, over large areas, you will have to join pieces together.

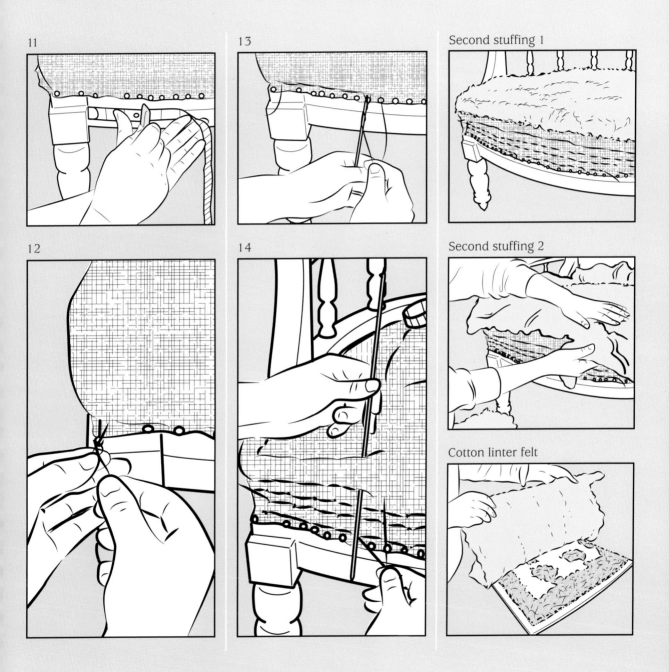

11

13

Second stuffing 1

12

14

Second stuffing 2

Cotton linter felt

Rubberised hair

Rubberised hair is a mix of hair and rubber supplied in sheet form. It's great for creating an immaculate look in minutes: instant gratification! Do make sure that the skin side faces up and the open side faces down. If you have complicated shapes to make – stuffing the inside of a wing or tub chair, for example – you can cut it using scissors and join pieces together with spray adhesive. You can then spray glue strips of calico along the joins to reinforce.

YOU WILL NEED

- Fibre
- Rubberised hair
- Scissors
- Staple gun
- Staples
- Stanley knife

- Spray adhesive
- Calico
- Nylon thread
- Black fibre
- Cotton felt

1 In this drop-in seat example, the aim is to have a slight dome just towards the front of centre. Position some fibre under the bridle ties then cover with rubberised hair.

2 Once the rubberised hair is in position over the fibre, staple it in place. Be sure to staple about 1.5–2.5cm (½–1in) away from the frame edge (leaving room for the following layer of felt).

3 Using a Stanley knife, trim close to your line of staples.

4 When the rubberised hair is in place, you can leave it as it is or shape it further with stuffing ties. This drop-in seat has a slight curve at the front so the stuffing should follow this line.

5 As after any first stuffing, you now need to bring the comfort back. With this drop-in seat, pieces of cotton felt are positioned over the dips made by the stuffing ties, then covered in a half-thickness layer of felt. (You can use double thickness too; it really depends on how thick you want the overall look and feel.) The seat is then finished with calico, followed by polyester and the top fabric.

TIPS

In this tub chair example, the ties pull the rubberised hair in and create that desirable curve. The tub chair needs to be constructed out of three pieces of rubberised hair. Position the central back piece and temporary tack. Then cut two more pieces and position on each side. As you reach the seat area, the rubberised hair will overlap. Mark, remove and cut the pieces. Lay the pieces of rubberised hair next to each other. Spray the edges of the pieces with spray adhesive, wait a minute, then bring them together. To firmly keep the pieces together, cut two strips of calico. Spray the rubberised hair and the calico with spray adhesive, wait a minute, then bring them together. Your stuffing is now ready to bring back to the chair. Once the rubberised hair is in place, permanently staple it and trim with a knife. Use stuffing ties to pull in the rubberised hair and bring back the shape of the tub. If you have a curve to follow, pleat or squeeze the rubberised hair around the curve rather than cutting the shape.

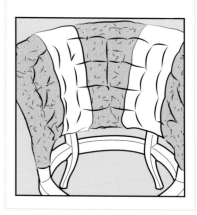

1

2

3

4

Foam

Foam is supplied in sheet form and cut to size; it comes in varying grades of firmness. The more you use foam, the more you'll get to know it. Your supplier will probably have a good idea about which you should buy to achieve the feel you're after. Reconstituted foam (chipfoam) is pretty tough and is mainly used in contract work, for bars and so on. It is commonly used for creating a firm edge, with a layer of softer foam added to bring back the comfort.

CUTTING

If you have a specific shape that needs to be cut, make a template for your foam supplier using paper – dot and cross is probably best. If you need to make any small alterations at home, use an electric carving knife. Constantly check that you are cutting straight in all directions. You can also buy tabletop cutters that will ensure an even cut. In most cases, it's best to cut slightly larger than your seat; you want the foam to fill out the cover, as it will lose shape over time and could cause the fabric to ripple.

ATTACHING

Gluing is a good method for attaching foam to foam, and foam to seat. Apply spray adhesive to both surfaces, wait a minute for the glue to become tacky and bring the two surfaces together. Make sure you are in a well-ventilated area and that you are using a dustsheet that you don't mind getting sticky.

As well as gluing you can also staple the foam in place. Where the foam hits the frame edge, just push down and let the staple pinch the foam and frame together. Any indents made by the staples will be filled when you cover with wadding.

DOMING

If you're intending to cover large areas with foam, for a day bed for example, you'll want to create a slight dome. If you don't, the large expanse of fabric will start to sag and ripple over time. You need to fill out areas in the same way that you would slightly overcut the foam for a box cushion (see page 80).

WALLING – MAKING A FIRM EDGE

To make a firm edge, for example on a tufted stool, cut the softer piece of foam to cover the stool, minus about 5cm (2in). Cut 5cm (2in) strips of reconstituted foam and spray glue to the edges of the foam.

If you use reconstituted foam for your seat, you can cover it in a thin layer of soft foam. This will mean the seat keeps a good shape, but is also comfortable for the sitter.

FINISHING

You should always cover foam in a layer of polyester wadding or stockinette. If you don't, the fabric will stick to the foam and cause friction. The fabric should glide over the foam rather than stick to it.

Polyester wadding

YOU WILL NEED
- Polyester wadding
- Scissors
- Spray adhesive

Polyester (poly) wadding is commonly used as a lining between the foam and the top cover. If it is used as a lining in conjunction with traditional materials though, it will not keep any stray hair or fibre from coming through the top cover. It's a cheaper alternative to some of the natural fillings and is also moisture resistant, so it will not rot.

1 Polyester wadding can be ripped in one direction, but is easier cut in the other. Measure and cut a piece and lay it over the foam. When you hit a corner, temporary tack the poly wadding so that it tightly covers the foam and the excess hangs at the corner.

2 Trim back the polyester overhang at the corner.

3 Spray the cut poly edges with spray adhesive. Leave for a minute, then squeeze together so that the foam is completely enveloped. Continue with your top cover.

Cutting

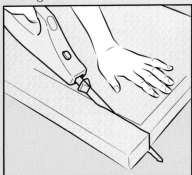

Doming

Polyester wadding 3

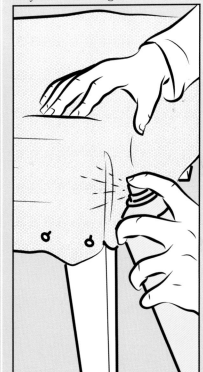

Attaching foam: glue

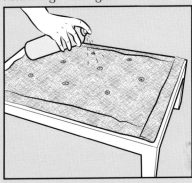

Polyester wadding 1

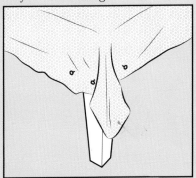

Attaching foam: staple

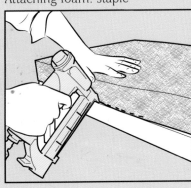

Polyester wadding 2

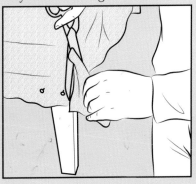

TIPS

It is best not to staple the wadding in position, as the top cover will be stretched over it and you want the wadding to move. Do not let the polyester excess turn under the frame with the top fabric. When you staple under the frame, lumps of poly will be visible rather than a crisp frame line.

Marianne Songbird

Marianne calls herself songbird – or rather that's the name of her blog – because 'nesting' is one of her biggest hobbies. She started her blog in 2008 and quickly found herself absorbed in a world of creative kindred spirits. *Songbirdblog* focuses on decoration and craft, with a leaning towards vintage-inspired thrifting. Marianne lives in the Netherlands.

FOR TUTORIALS
Stripping & cleaning: page 96
Painting a frame: page 100
Drop-in seat: page 72
The finishing touches: page 172

Having spent part of my life as a graphic designer, I found myself drawn to the bold typography on Marianne's chairs. The use of twine as a finishing partners well with the natural feel of the postage sacks. Having more show wood on display gives the chair a much better outline than before. And whether it's down to the positioning of the type on the postage bag or not, I really like the off-kilter feel.

BEFORE   AFTER

CHAIR STYLE
1955 dining-room chairs.

FABRIC USED
Reclaimed postal bags.

ORIGINAL STATE
Some repairs needed to the frame.
Seats needed to be replaced.

CHANGES MADE
Repaired and re-painted the frame.
Changed the stuffing.

TIME SPENT
About one week in total.

The chairs originally belonged to Marianne's parents and were bought as a dining-room set, including a table, in 1955. When her mother passed away, Marianne agreed with her siblings that the chairs would be sent to the local dump. Marianne explains, 'As I saw the cart with all the stuff leave, a lump formed in my throat and I felt a brick in my stomach. I just couldn't let it happen, my mum's beloved furniture discarded like that.' Having rescued them in the nick of time, the chairs spent years sat in the basement, along with the table. Eventually, inspired by the blogging community, Marianne took up her tools and tackled the first of the chairs.

She was faced with an unbelievable amount of nails to remove. This stage can be very disheartening when all you want to do is get to the good bit – the fabric. She improvised with her tools and employed a screwdriver to remove the nails before investing in a specialist tool for the second chair. A sound investment. She filled the holes with liquid wood, then sanded, primed and painted the frame.

> *The chair is not perfect in any way, but I think it is beautiful and it is a constant and lovely reminder of my mother. I know she would have loved that I made the chair my own and that I did that project by myself too*

A local upholsterer gave her some advice regarding the process and materials. They even drew her a sketch and gave a few tips, rather than just offering their services.

Marianne kept the old fabric to use as a template for the following layers. The springs had originally been covered with hessian and pieces of carpet. Marianne thankfully chose to remove and replace this with some new burlap. She made sure there was a gap left between the edge of the hessian and the edge of the frame. Leaving a gap means that you have somewhere for the following layers to be fixed.

She then roughly cut some foam to size and placed it onto the seat. With a marker pen, she marked around the frame on the underside. The upholsterer had told her to use a wide pen so that the foam she cut would be about 1.5cm (½in) wider than the seat, allowing for the foam to ease over the edge. She cut the foam with a carving knife and covered it with fibrefill (poly wadding or batting) and glued it to the edge of the seat. Some masking tape was then positioned around the seat so that the fabric would stop on a straight line. For the back, Marianne attached some white foam, realising that if you stapled the top followed by the bottom then repeated this, it was easier to keep the curved shape of the back. Having given the bags a good wash, she covered and stapled them in place, finishing by attaching the twine with fabric glue.

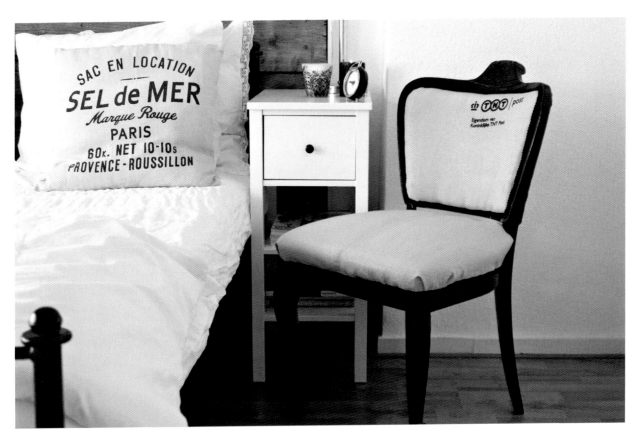

Later, Marianne tackled another of the chairs with some slightly newer mail bags, finishing with some black lacy ribbon. The process this time was much easier as she knew what to expect.

I look forward to the last two chairs being completed and posted on her blog – and what about that table?

Measuring & cutting

It's a good idea to make a cutting plan for your fabric – professional upholsterers will always do this. If you have a penchant for buying expensive fabric, knowing exactly how much you need is an especially good thing.

TIPS
If your fabric is expensive or you only have a limited amount, you can add a fly to the areas of your chair that are concealed, thereby using less of your favoured fabric (see page 166).

Measuring a chair

YOU WILL NEED
• Tape measure
• Pen and paper

The diagram opposite shows you how to label the sections of a chair, which is useful if you're cutting a few pieces at a time and don't want to be left with a confusing pile of fabric.

Measuring

YOU WILL NEED
• Tape measure
• Pen and paper

1 Measure the chair while it's still upholstered. If you're planning to rip your chair down and restuff the seat 30cm (12in) higher than before or are making any other dramatic size and shape changes, take these into account when measuring.

2 To measure the seat, start from under the front seat rail, then go over the seat, push the tape between the seat and the inside back and under the back rail – accounting for enough to pull on. Note that you will have to undo the bottom of the outside back to do this. Remember to take the measurement at the widest point in each of the areas.

Making a cutting plan

YOU WILL NEED
• Pen and paper

1 Draw out the fabric (on paper) and piece the panels together. Note: there are many 'rules' in upholstery and one such rule refers to fabric direction. The arrows on the diagram opposite show this rule. However, rules are made to be broken; if you're using a fabric with a pattern that is more pleasing to the eye running from front to back on the arms as well as the seat, then go with it. Just remember that if you are using a fabric with a deep pile such as velvet, it's best to stick to the rule, as velvet changes colour when viewed from different directions.

2 When you've positioned all your panels and accounted for piping, you'll now know how much fabric to order.

Working with pattern repeats

When buying fabric with a pattern, you'll need to know the size of the pattern repeat. This measurement will be referred to in the fabric details. If you already have your fabric, you can check this measurement yourself. Choose a point in the design near the selvage, then measure down the length of fabric until you reach the same point. Do the same across the width. These measurements are the pattern repeat.

Unless you're experimenting or making a design statement, it's best to match up the centre lines on the outside back, inside back and seat.

Measuring a chair

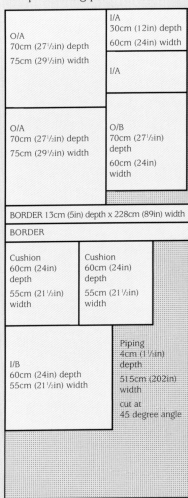

IB = Inside back

IA = Inside arm x2

PF = Seat platform front

OB = Outside back

OA = Outside arm x2

C = Cushions x2

CB = Cushion border

Sample cutting plan

	I/A 30cm (12in) depth 60cm (24in) width
O/A 70cm (27½in) depth 75cm (29½in) width	I/A
O/A 70cm (27½in) depth 75cm (29½in) width	O/B 70cm (27½in) depth 60cm (24in) width

BORDER 13cm (5in) depth x 228cm (89in) width

BORDER

Cushion 60cm (24in) depth 55cm (21½in) width	Cushion 60cm (24in) depth 55cm (21½in) width	
I/B 60cm (24in) depth 55cm (21½in) width		Piping 4cm (1½in) depth 515cm (202in) width cut at 45 degree angle

Haley Beham

Haley works for a travel company by day and is a photographer by night and at weekends. She is a lover of projects, all of which she documents in her blog, *The Daily Haley*. The blog started out as a way to update family and friends on progress made in the house she shares with her husband Matthew in San Antonio, Texas.

FOR TUTORIALS
Stripping a wooden frame: page 96
Painting a wooden frame: page 100
Drop-in seat: page 72
The finishing touches: page 172

BEFORE   AFTER

Every aspect of this chair works. Overall it's well proportioned with gently tapered legs and soft curves. The grey/yellow colour combination and the use of cotton webbing as a backing are inspired and original. Haley opted to keep the look and feel of a woven back, but using an unexpected material.

She spotted the chair among neighbourhood cast-offs left out as rubbish. Rather than an intricate pattern of woven cane, the back was just a gaping hole and the cushion ripped to shreds, but Haley could see the potential, deciding to focus her attention on the structure of the chair as a whole and not be put off by the tattiness of the upholstery.

Finding the time and inspiration to work on the chair took a further three years, in which time the chair moved from garage to garden, and also to a new house. Eventually she set to work, beginning by removing the frayed cane from the frame. She then prepped the chair for painting – a dull job that accounted for much of her time. Haley's chair is testament to the '5 per cent decoration, 95 per cent preparation' adage. After countless rounds of filling and sanding, Haley sprayed the chair with an oil-based primer, followed by four coats of paint. For that ultra-smooth professional finish, she finely sanded between coats and sealed it with polyurethane.

I had big, big intentions of making this chair beautiful. I just had to find the time and the inspiration

CHAIR STYLE
Early 20th century-style carver chair.

FABRIC
Lovesme Lovesmenot in Golden by Anna Maria Horner.

ORIGINAL STATE
A total wreck! The caning in the back was completely shot and the cushion was shredded.

CHANGES MADE
The frame was painted. The caning was replaced with cotton webbing. A new drop-in seat was fitted – both filling and cover.

TIME SPENT
Twelve hours.

Once the chair was dry, Haley webbed the back. She fixed the vertical webs in place with upholstery nails, stapling at the base once everything was woven. When she reached the curved area in the back, she used a continuous piece of web for both the horizontals and verticals.

The seat is of a drop-in construction, the base a piece of plywood supported by corner blocks inside the seat frame. Hayley replaced the original foam. Wanting the same thickness but not finding it on sale, she layered and glued a few pieces together with spray adhesive. She covered the foam with wadding, stapled it to the plywood, covered it in the fabric and stapled again.

Clearly Haley succeeded in her mission to make the chair beautiful. 'I love how the chair turned out overall. It is incredibly comfortable! I think if I had it to do again, I might not wait three years before getting started on it!'

Sarah Whyberd

Sarah Whyberd is a London-based designer maker, with a love for sewing and gorgeous fabrics. Since her childhood spent in rural Cumbria, Sarah has always been surrounded by homemade things whether it's freshly baked cakes, handmade cushions or hand-knitted jumpers.

FOR TUTORIALS
Rubberised hair: page 130
Piping: page 160
Bringing it all together: page 164

BEFORE   AFTER

These 1950s Encore chairs were designed by Howard Keith, the British furniture designer who founded HK Furniture in the 1930s. This pair originally belonged to Sarah's great-grandmother, but spent their latter years in her parents' conservatory. Although they were in good condition, still in the original moquette fabric, they were in urgent need of an update.

While ripping down the chair, Sarah discovered the rubberised hair was still holding up well and could be re-used. The spring unit, however, was beyond repair. After struggling to find a supplier for a replacement, Sarah decided to construct a new unit using pieces of the old one. She then made a hessian cover and blanket stitched it to the unit. The old rubberised hair was re-positioned and stapled to the back and a new layer added to the seat. This was then covered in a layer of felt and wadding before the top cover. For the back, a new layer of hessian was tacked into place, covered in wadding and some linen was hand-stitched in place.

When choosing fabric, Sarah always takes inspiration from the chair's beginnings and its story. She remembered how her great-grandmother would use fabric again and again. When new curtains were made for the house, a dress would be made to match! The velvet curtains that had hung in Sarah's bedroom in her family home were now redundant, so she decided to re-purpose this fabric in the same way her great-grandmother would have done. 'I don't know the name of the fabric – we always referred to it as the Birds of Paradise. It originally came from the Stead McAlpin Mill just outside Carlisle in the 1950s.' With limited curtain fabric available, Sarah sourced some green coarse linen to use for piping and on the back of the chairs. Texturally the linen is a great contrast, but it also modernises the vintage velvet.

With hindsight, Sarah thinks she should have 'backed' the fabric to strengthen it. The curtains were quite difficult to work with because the fabric had become quite delicate with age. Successfully pulling the fabric taut without ripping it was a challenge. However, Sarah knew that these chairs would be show pieces and not used day in day out, so the strength of the fabric would not be a major problem once they were finished. The chairs have great sentimental value for Sarah and are sure to become a much loved heirloom in the future.

CHAIR STYLE
1950s Howard Keith Encore chairs.

FABRIC USED
Re-purposed curtains: vintage fabric originally sourced from the Stead McAlpin Mill near Carlisle, UK. Green linen from The Cloth Shop on Portobello Road, London.

ORIGINAL STATE
The chairs were still holding together in the original moquette, but needed an update.

CHANGES MADE
The chairs were completely stripped down. A new spring unit was created out of the original one.

TIME SPENT
Approximately ten days.

As there were two chairs and limited fabric, I had to find a contrasting fabric for the backs and piping. Having tried many different samples, a green linen seemed to be the perfect thing. I liked the way it gave another texture and I think it also modernises the velvet

Calico & cuts

The following pages show you how to position the calico and the top cover and make any necessary cuts.

Calico

Before adding the top cover, you'll need to add a layer of calico. Using calico gives you a good idea of the finished look. It will also take the strain of the many layers of stuffing so there'll be less wear on your top cover, and if you're worried about making cuts, the calico layer provides an opportunity to practise.

The top cover

You should aim to get your calico – and, more importantly, your top fabric – as taut as you can and as close to any obstacles as possible. What you don't want are gaping holes and exposed stuffing. As for cutting the top cover, the process is identical to calico – just be sure to add a further layer of stuffing. Remember, if you've stuffed with coir or hair you'll need to use either skin wadding or cotton linter felt to keep those hairs from protruding. If you're unsure of the cut you need to make, use a scrap piece of calico first.

Order of work

1. The calico on the arms and back need to be permanently fixed to the outside of the back and arm stuffing rail.

2. Temporary tack the top cover.

3. Once the seat is in place, the top cover will be fixed to the top of the side and back stretcher rails and under the front stretcher rail.

4. You then bring down the top cover on the arms and back and fix it over the top of the seat fabric.

Positioning calico

YOU WILL NEED
- Tape measure
- Scissors
- Calico
- Tacks
- Tailor's chalk

1 Measure your seat, arm or back and cut some calico to fit. Position it so that the threads run straight from front to back and left to right.

2 Temporary tack the calico onto the back stuffing rail. Smooth your hand over the calico from front to back while gently pulling down at the front with your other hand. Repeat on the sides of the chair. Make sure the fabric is positioned correctly before making any cuts.

3 Fold the calico or fabric back on itself and mark any cutting lines on the reverse. (You'll probably need to remove some of the temporary tacks to do this).

Measuring cuts

To cut correctly you need to measure the width of the upright you are cutting around, then measure the distance between the upright and the fabric. This will give you your cutting stop point. To do this, you can use a measuring tape and a regulator as a guide.

Making cuts

YOU WILL NEED
- Regulator
- Tailor's chalk
- Tape measure
- Scissors

1 Push the flat end of the regulator into the gap between the seat and the arm. Keep it up close to the edge of the upright. Using chalk, mark a line along the inside edge of the regulator onto the calico or top cover. Repeat on the other side of the upright.

2 Bring the end of the regulator or tape measure up to where the upright meets the stuffing. Measure from this point to the edge of the folded fabric. With this measurement, mark from the foldback and draw a line. This line is where your cut should stop. You should now have three lines on the reverse of the calico or top fabric.

Positioning calico 2

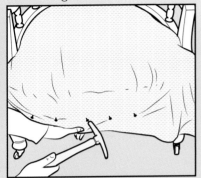

Positioning calico 3

Making cuts 1

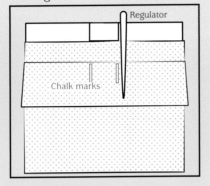

Making cuts 2

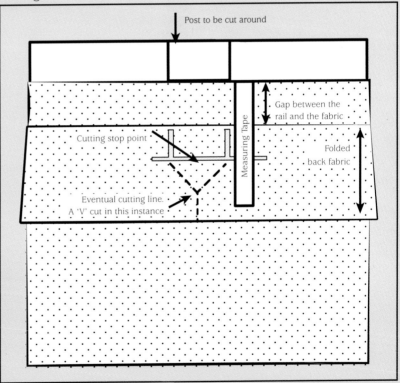

TIPS

Before making any cuts, take a good look at the space the fabric needs to fill. You want to have surplus fabric on either side of the leg or arm upright that can be neatly folded under. If you miss this stage out, you might be left with exposed stuffing.

Make one set of cuts at a time. For all areas, make the cuts at the back first, temporary tack in place, then make the cuts at the front.

Calico & cuts

'V' cut

YOU WILL NEED
- Tape measure
- Scissors
- Regulator
- Tacks

The 'V' cut is a common cut for an upright with a flat edge. It looks like a 'Y' because of the initial straight cut, but it is actually a 'V'. This cut leaves you with an equal amount of fabric on either side of the upright that you can fold away.

1 Fold the calico back so that it is flat on the seat with the right sides together. Measure where your cut should stop. Cut straight to the middle of the upright, stopping a couple of centimetres or so away from the stop mark.

2 Make a cut on the left, stopping at the point where the two marks meet.

3 Repeat step 2 on the right to create the 'V' shape.

4 Bring the fabric back under the rails and check the cut. If all looks good, tuck the surplus 'V'-shaped fabric down under the calico using the regulator.

5 Working from the outside of the chair, fold under the surplus fabric so that the fold butts up to the leg. Tack in place.

Cutting to a corner upright

YOU WILL NEED
- Regulator
- Scissors

1 Fold back the fabric so that the fold is at a 45-degree angle to the corner. If the upright is exposed, butt the fold right up to the corner. If not, use your regulator to measure where your cut will end.

2 Cut straight up to the corner of the upright, but stop just short of it. This allows the fabric to sink into any fillings between the upright and the top of the seat.

3 Take each piece of fabric from either side of the cut around the stump. Use the regulator to tuck in any fabric.

4 Fold under the surplus fabric and fix in position.

Cutting around an arm

YOU WILL NEED
- Regulator
- Tailor's chalk
- Scissors

There are two rails that need to be cut around at the back of the arm: a 'Y' at the top and a 'V' at the bottom. A 'Y' cut leaves you with more fabric on one side of the cut than the other. In this case, more fabric will be given to the outside arm. So there's more fabric to play with in case of any cutting slip ups.

1 Make sure the calico is secured in position. Release a few tacks at the back and fold the fabric away from the back rail.

2 Use the regulator to locate and mark the positioning and width of the rails.

3 Make the 'Y' cut at the top and take the fabric over the top of the arm and secure it on the back post (as per illustration). Now cut the short part of the 'Y' in the opposite direction (a reverse of the 'Y' you have just cut). This will enable you to move the fabric around the arm rail and bring it through to the outside arm.

4 Make the 'V' cut where the fabric hits the arm and back stuffing rail. Take the fabric under the arm stuffing rail and secure to the outside of the arm stretcher rails. Note that your arm top fabric will eventually be permanently stapled over the top fabric for the seat. Take the loose fabric at the back of the arm through the gap between the arm rail and the arm stuffing rail. Secure to the outside arm using skewers. Note: the calico and the top cover for the back of the chair are also pulled through this gap. Secure the back fabric onto the back post. Remove the skewers from the arm fabric and secure over the top of the back fabric.

V cut 1

V cut 2

V cut 3

V cut 5

Cutting to corner upright 3

Cutting around an arm 4

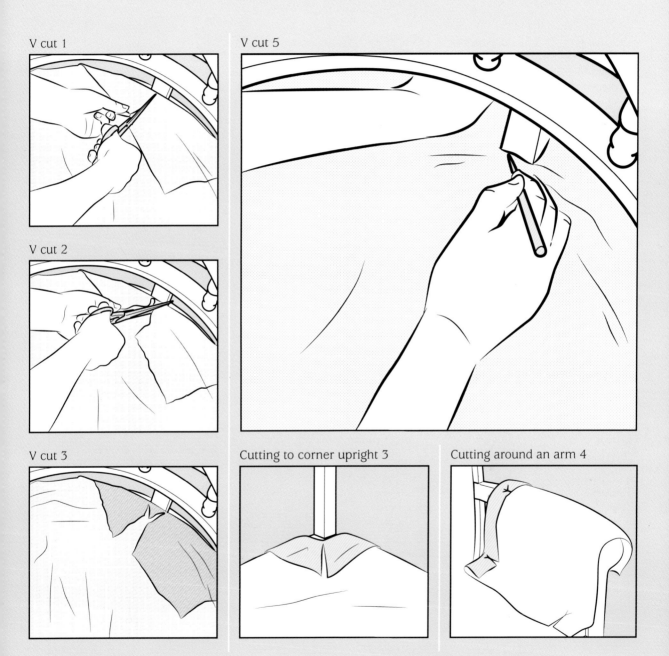

Joining fabric: tub chair

A tub chair, as the name suggests, has an inner curve with what looks like – and can even be, if you're a miracle worker – one continuous piece of fabric. Generally, though, the inside of a tub chair is made up of three pieces of fabric. In the example shown here, each piece is shown with a piped seam for strength and decoration.

YOU WILL NEED
- Piping
- Fabric
- Scissors
- Tape measure
- Tailor's chalk
- Marker pen (optional)
- Sewing machine
- Staple gun or hammer and tacks

1 Temporary tack a length of piping cord on the outside arm rail next to the back leg uprights. Take the cord up between the seat and inside back and temporary tack on the top rail. How you position these will be a matter of visual judgement, and also a prediction of how your fabric might fall – you don't want ripples. Stand back and adjust by eye until you are happy. Mark the line with some chalk and remove the cord.

2 Measure and cut three pieces of fabric for the back and two inside arms. Cut a notch at the top and bottom centres of your back piece. Also mark the frame. Position and temporary tack the fabric in place. When you are happy, fold back each piece along the chalked line and pin in place. Make the necessary release cuts to help guide the fabric along the line.

3 Measure a 1.5cm (½in) seam allowance back from the fold on each piece and trim.

4 Mark the seam allowance at intervals and cut a notch. This will help you reassemble the pieces later. Also mark the positioning of the fabric on the frame.

5 Remove the pieces from the chair and reassemble with the piping between each seam. At this point you might want to hand tack together before running the fabric through the sewing machine. Machine all three together with a 1.5cm (½in) seam allowance.

6 Add a layer of skin or polyester wadding to the inside of your chair. Reposition the sewn fabric pieces on the chair and temporary tack in place. Cut the fabric around the legs and temporary tack onto the back and arm stuffing rails. Once your top fabric is in position on the seat, you can permanently tack or staple over this onto the back and side stretcher rail.

1

2

3

4

5

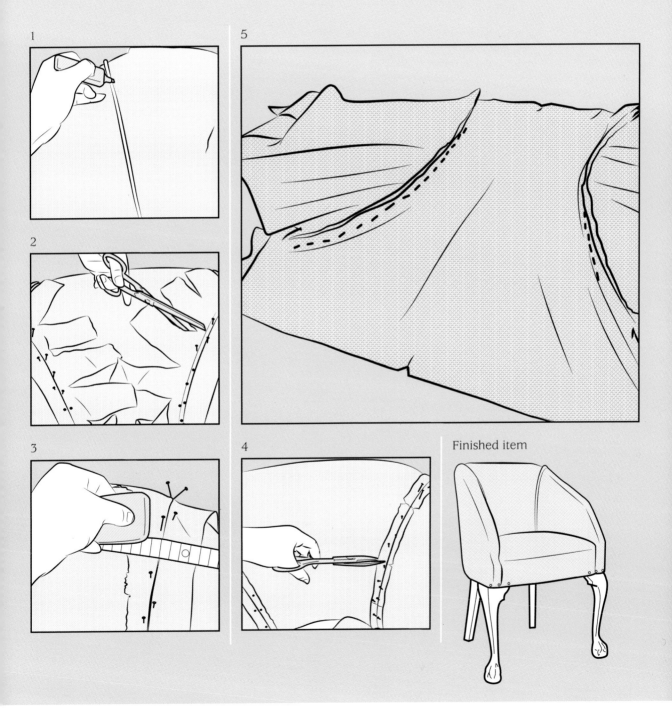

Finished item

Scroll arm with pleats

As you wrap fabric around arms or over corners there's bound to be some excess. Lose this with a combination of tucking away, cutting and folding into pleats. The example on these pages shows simple pleats on a scroll arm; this technique works well on very delicate arms. If you need to cover larger arms you can finish the pleats at the centre of the front post and cover with a facing (see page 156). Whichever style you choose, make sure the folds face inwards and both arms match.

YOU WILL NEED
- Scissors
- Pins
- Regulator
- Hammer and tacks or staple gun

Have your fabric temporary tacked in position with the cuts around uprights completed (see page 146). Make sure that the fabric is also tacked in place on the underside of the arm rail. The only loose piece of fabric that you want is around the scroll itself.

1 Pull the fabric around the front of the arm and tack in place on the outside of the arm.

2 Make a diagonal cut up to where the arm upright becomes a scroll. Stop just short. This will release the loose fabric around the scroll from the taut fabric around the bottom of the arm.

3 As you begin wrapping the fabric around the scroll, you should feel where the first pleat needs to start. Pull down the first pleat and fold directly into the corner where the scroll meets the arm (where you made the cut in step 1).

4 Continue manipulating the fabric around the top of the arm curve. Make neat folds that finish in the same corner. Use the flat end of the regulator to help you make these folds. Try to make each pleat the same size. You might need to practise this part without tacking in place first. When you are happy with the pleats, temporary tack or pin each fold in place.

5 You might be left with some fabric that won't fold into a pleat. This is normal! To lose this piece, fold so that the fold edge faces out at the front of the chair. When you're happy, permanently staple or tack in place.

TIPS

To make a scroll arm with a facing: finish any folds you make towards the centre of the front upright. These will be covered by the facing.

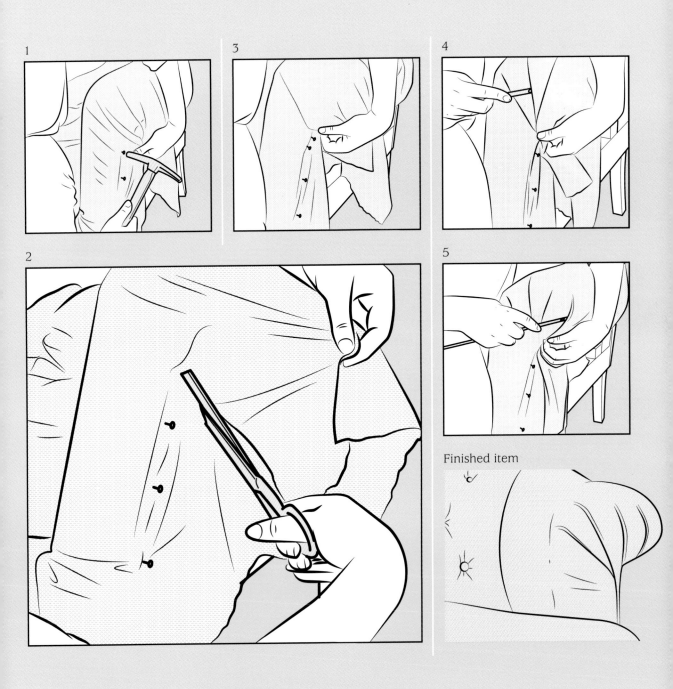

Finished item

Corners

So, you've reached the corner of your seat and there is quite a bit of excess fabric left that you need to do something with. The 'look' you want for your finished chair will dictate how you fold away this fabric. A single pleat will give you a sharp, box-like look while a double pleat will give a more rounded effect.

> **TIPS**
> It's a good idea to practise steps 2 and 3 before stapling, as these techniques can be tricky.

Single pleat corner

YOU WILL NEED
- Calico or top cover
- Staple gun
- Staples
- Scissors
- Upholstery hammer
- Tacks

1 With the frame on its side, pull the calico from the opposite side of the corner over the corner towards you.

2 Staple the calico on the edge facing you.

3 Hold the calico on the edge nearest to you and make a fold that sits in line with the edge of the corner. When you're happy with the positioning, cut away any excess fabric that could potentially bulk up the seat.

4 Fold the pleat over and fasten with tacks.

Double pleat corner

YOU WILL NEED
- Calico or top cover
- Upholstery hammer
- Tacks
- Staple gun
- Staples
- Scissors

1 Pull the fabric at the corner and take it under the frame at a 45-degree angle to the underside edges – temporary tack it in place. Make sure there are equal amounts of fabric on either side of the tack.

2 Move the fabric on either side of the tack clear. Staple on either side of the tack on the underside rail. Remove the temporary tack and trim back any surplus fabric. Start to make your pleats on either side of the corner – they should be a mirror image of each other. Try to finish each pleat close to the corner.

3 When you're happy with the pleats, bring one side down and under the frame. Permanently staple in place.

4 Note: if you are making a corner pleat for a stuffed chair seat whose legs are right on the corner (see finished item illustration), staple the pleats as close to the bottom of the seat as possible. Then cover any staples with double piping, trim or upholstery nails.

Single pleat 1

Single pleat 4

Double pleat 2

Single pleat 2

Single pleat finished item

Double pleat 3

Single pleat 3

Double pleat 1

Double pleat finished item

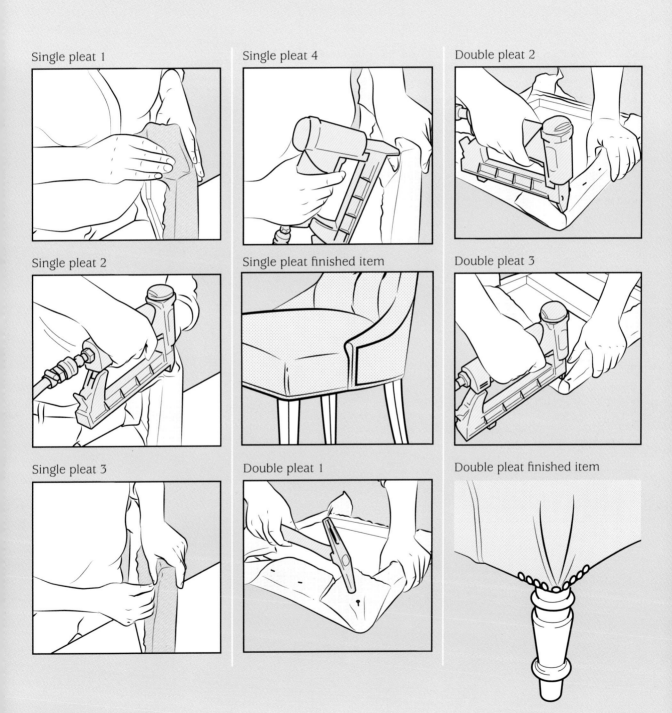

Machined corner seam

It is possible with much modern furniture to pre-machine corners, facing and arms, then simply slide onto the piece of furniture. This works especially well if the shape you are covering is solid. The example shown here is a machined corner of a stool with a very square edge. The base is webbed and covered with hessian. I cut a piece of foam just proud of the edges and used spray adhesive to glue it in place. See page 132 for more on using foam.

YOU WILL NEED
- Top cover fabric
- Tape measure
- Scissors
- Tailor's chalk
- Polyester wadding
- Yard stick
- Sewing machine
- Pins

TIPS

It's always good practice to mark centre points on both fabric and chair. This is especially important if the upholstery involves the removal and sewing of fabric.

1 Measure the stool exactly from the base on one side to the other. Add an extra 3cm (1¼in) on all sides. This will give you enough fabric for pulling, bringing under the base and stapling. Cut your fabric.

2 Mark the centre points on the front and back rail of the stool. Lay out the fabric face down and mark the centre points on the front and back of that as well.

3 Measure the height of the stool. Add 3cm (1¼in) to this measurement. Using your yard stick and some tailor's chalk, mark this measurement up and across the corner of your fabric. Repeat this process on the remaining three corners.

4 Mark a 1.5cm (¾in) seam allowance in towards the corner from both your original marks.

5 Cut along the seam allowances and remove the square of fabric. Bring the two cut edges together and pin along the original marks made in step 3.

6 Sometimes the completed corner can have a 'dog-eared' look. To overcome this, mark and machine a slight diagonal towards the corner away from the seam.

7 Machine together. Repeat steps 4 to 7 on the remaining three corners. Turn the fabric right side out. You should now be left with what looks like a box lid.

8 Cover the foam with some polyester wadding. Fit the wadding snug to the foam. Cut the corners and glue. Trim along the base of the frame. See page 132 for more on using polyester wadding. Slip the cover over the stool. Line up centre points and staple on the underside of the stool. At this point you can add some decorative nails, trim or floating buttons. See page 172 for finishing touches and page 168 for tufting.

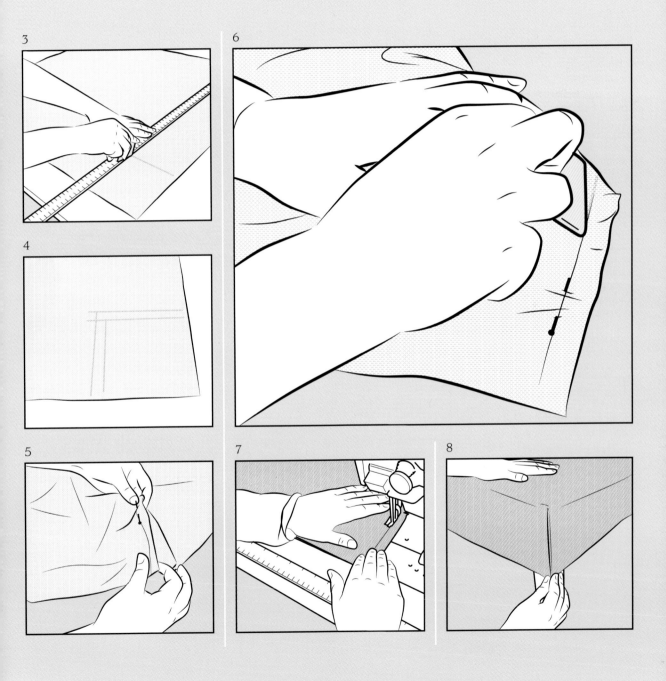

3

4

5

6

7

8

Facing

In this example a piped facing is covered and attached to a wing-back chair. Make scroll arm pleats as before (see page 150), but this time direct the folds to the centre of the arm scroll. If you broke the facing when you ripped down the chair, have them cut by your local timber merchant using some thin plywood.

There are a couple of ways of attaching the newly upholstered facing. For example, you could pre-drill some holes and use a plastic clip fastening. One half is ready-inserted into the front upright, the other through the uncovered facing. Once the facing is covered, you simply line up the fastener and hammer it home. Another method is to cover the facing and use small-headed panel pins through the top cover. This method only works if you have an open-weave fabric. Once the facing is nailed into place the fabric is worked – using the regulator – on top of the nail head.

Covering with fabric

YOU WILL NEED
- Piping
- Wooden or cardboard facing
- Tailor's chalk
- Scissors
- Polyester wadding
- Staple gun
- Staples
- Hammer

1 Make up enough piping to fit around the facing, with a bit extra. Lay the wooden or cardboard facing face down onto the wrong side of some fabric. Draw around the shape with about 2.5cm (1in) excess. Where the bottom of the curve hits the straight edge, leave the fabric long. This edge will eventually be attached to the outside edge of the front upright.

2 Cut some polyester wadding to size and place it between the cover and the facing board. Fold the fabric at the top of the board over and staple on the reverse, then repeat at the opposite end. When these areas are secure, continue stapling the outer edges of the board. Don't staple on the uncut side. Do not overstretch the fabric as any pattern on it will be distorted. You want it to be tight, but not stretched.

3 Make a straight cut in from the edge to the point where the curve of the facing begins. Continue to staple around the curve up to this cut.

4 Position the piping with the seam allowance on the reverse and the actual piped edge firmly resting against the edge of the facing. You might need to make some cuts and remove some fabric from the piping seam allowance, as this will likely be lumpy. Staple in place again, leaving the uncut edge free.

5 Now position onto the front of the arm upright and hammer in position. Depending on how tight the facing is to the arm you might want to finish with a slip stitch between the facing, through the piping and into the scroll arm.

6 Take the loose side of fabric onto the outside back and staple on the outside of the front post.

7 Bring the piping down to the stretcher rail. Keep straight and staple in place. Eventually the outside arm will be slip stitched to this piping.

Piped flat facing

With piped flat facing, use the technique for joining fabric on page 148. Do all the measuring and cutting before the addition of the final layer of wadding. This will mean that your finished sewn join will be tight to the chair arm.

Curved facing

On some wing chairs, the facing is slightly curved and surrounded by piping. In this case, attach piping all the way around. Work out where the piping cord meets and trim the cord, leaving some fabric free. Fold under the end of the fabric and cover the other edge of piping, then continue to staple in place.

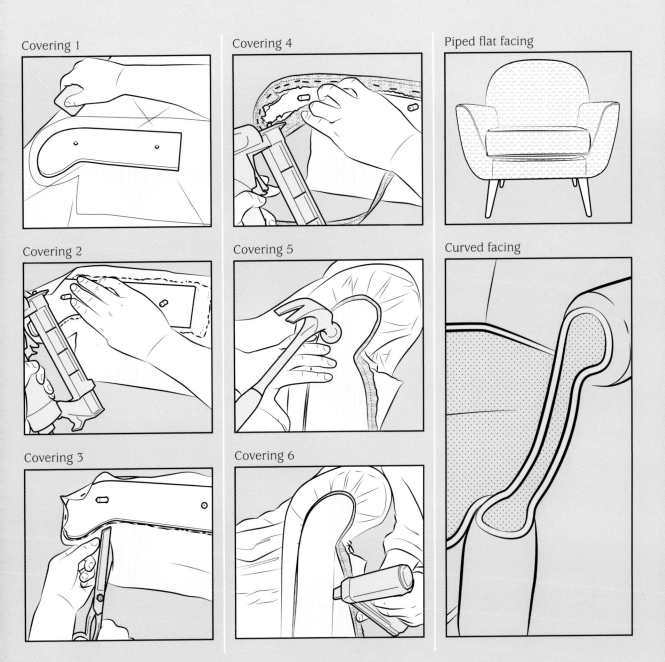

Covering 1

Covering 2

Covering 3

Covering 4

Covering 5

Covering 6

Piped flat facing

Curved facing

Borders

In the same way as adding a facing (see page 156), the addition of a border is down to personal taste or the style of the chair.

YOU WILL NEED
- Tape measure
- Piping
- Pins
- Wadding
- Curved needle
- Staples/tacks
- Scissors

TIPS
If your chair had a border when you ripped it down, it doesn't necessarily need to be reinstated. You can always just bring the fabric over the seat and down under the front rail.

1 Measure the border panel with extra fabric for pulling. Make up some piping and pin along one edge of the border.

2 Position the sewn border along the front of the seat. Pin in place. Position some wadding under the border.

3 Temporary tack the bottom of the border to the underside of the front stretcher rail. With a curved needle, slip stitch the border in place – as always, one stitch through the border, up through the piping, then one stitch on the seat. Repeat.

4 Continue stitching to the edges of the chair. Temporary tack on the outside of the chair on the front post.

5 Gently pull down from the piping and permanently staple or tack under the front stretcher rail, making any necessary cuts around the legs.

6 In this example, the arms are treated in the same way as the front border. The front seat border is completed and permanently stapled to the outside arm on each side. The inside and outside arms are then upholstered and stapled to the top of the arms. A strip of fabric is cut for the top arm border and some piping machine-stitched to each side. The arm border is then positioned and hand slip stitched into place.

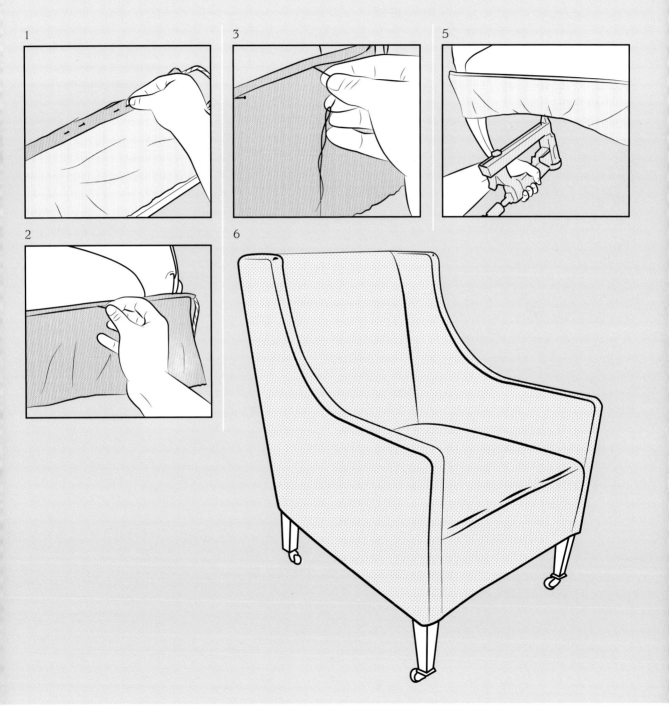

Piping

Piping is used to give strength to seams that receive a lot of wear and also to give that professional 'finished' look. This is also your chance to play with contrasting or complementary colours that will really stand out. Spend some time choosing the right fabric – pin a couple of samples to the chair and stand back. Experiment with using different colours or sizes of piping. Think carefully about how much piping to use – if you are piping a cushion as well as the arms, the facing and the back, your finished chair could suffer from piping overkill. In the end, though, the decision comes down to your own personal taste.

Single piping

YOU WILL NEED
- Piping fabric
- Ruler
- Tailor's chalk
- Sewing machine with a piping or zipper foot
- Matching thread
- Scissors
- Regulator
- Piping cord

1 Lay out your fabric and, with a ruler, mark out lengths of piping across the bias. Fold the end of your fabric over and line up with the selvage to make a square. The fold will give you the 45-degree line. Cut your lengths 4cm (1½in) thick. Note: if you are making piping to match stripes, you'll need to cut the piping straight.

2 Measure how much piping you will need and machine stitch the lengths of fabric together. If you have cut your fabric on the bias, position the lengths together with right sides facing and mark with chalk as in illustration 2a. If you have straight-cut lengths, position them together with right sides facing and mark as in illustration 2b.

3 Machine stitch together along the line and trim.

4 Turn over and, using the flat edge of the regulator, press open the seam. If your fabric is pretty thick or if you have time, press the seam open with an iron.

5 Lay the piping cord centrally on the wrong side of the fabric and fold the left side over to meet with the right-hand edge. Holding them together as you go, run the lengths of fabric through the machine.

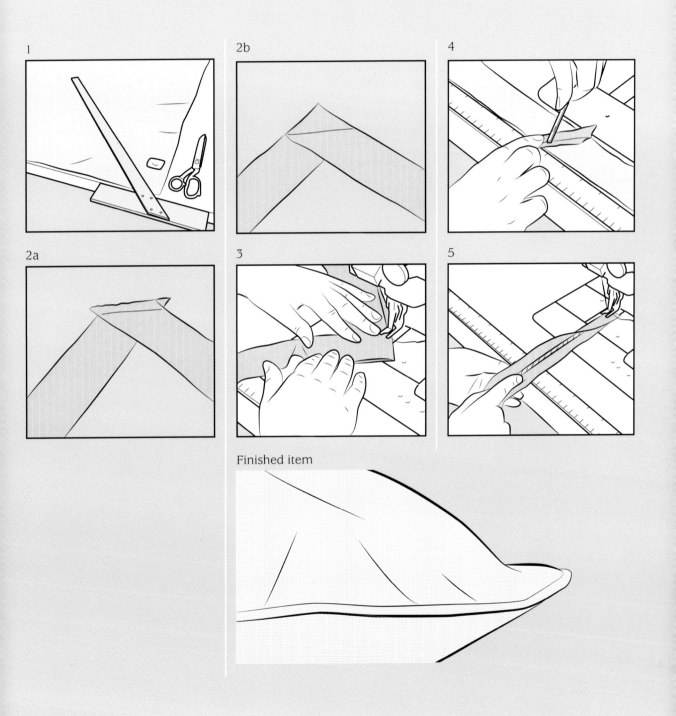

1

2a

2b

3

4

5

Finished item

Piping

YOU WILL NEED
- Piping fabric
- Ruler
- Tailor's chalk
- Scissors
- Matching thread
- Sewing machine with a double piping foot
- Piping cord
- Regulator (optional)

Double piping

Double piping is a great way to finish a piece of furniture. It's cheap, quick to make and if you use the same fabric as your chair, it will match perfectly. Run the piping along the bottom or edges of the chair to cover any visible staples or tacks. To attach it, simply use a combination of hot glue and coloured gimp pins.

1 As with single piping, measure how much fabric you will need. Cut the lengths 5cm (2in) thick. Machine stitch the lengths together, press the seam and trim.

2 Lay the cord on the wrong side of the fabric and fold the left side over, but not all the way to the opposite edge. At this point you can sew the cord in place. If you sew the first piece of cord in place, it means that you only need to concentrate on holding the fabric tight over the second piece of cord, rather than pushing the fabric from the left over the first cord and pushing to the right over the second cord.

3 Lay another length of cord alongside the first piece of piping and on top of the folded-over fabric.

4 Fold the fabric from the right over the cord, keeping both tightly together. This can be quite difficult, so practise with a scrap piece of fabric first.

5 Holding the two lengths of cord firmly together with the fabric pulled taut over the top, feed through the machine.

6 Trim off any surplus fabric from the back of the piping.

Double welt cord

Double welt cord is also available. If you're using double welt cord:

1 Wrap the fabric over the cord, hold it taut and sew between the piping cords with a straight stitch.

2 Roll the cord over in the fabric so that it is now completely covered.

3 Now put it back in the sewing machine and sew again with a straight stitch.

4 Cut off any excess fabric close to the seam.

Double piping 2

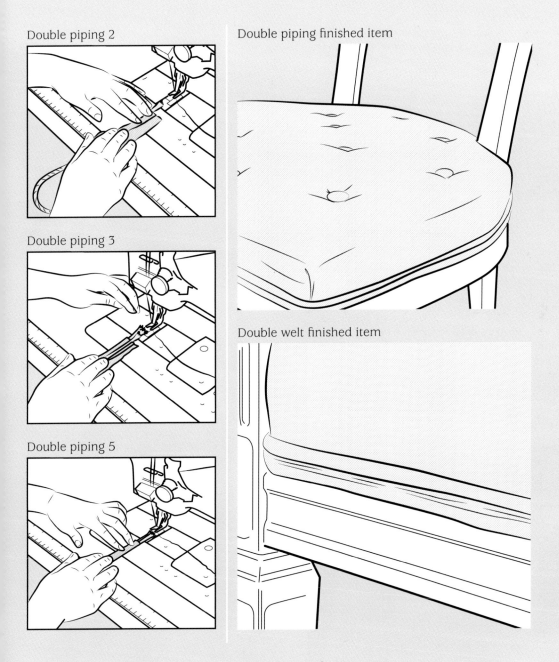

Double piping 3

Double piping 5

Double piping finished item

Double welt finished item

Bringing it all together

Everything's beginning to look good from the front, but there are still some finishing touches you need to make to ensure a really professional-looking job.

Tub chair piping

Joining the outside arms and back in the same way as the inside arms and back and lining up the piping on the outside back with the piping on the inside back can lead to a 'piping build-up'. Here's how to avoid this.

1 Work out where the outside back will sit on the piping. Open up the piping on the inside back to that line. Trim the piping.

2 Staple the piping from the inside back down. Run some piping around the outside back along the top of the chair and staple.

Outside back and arms

YOU WILL NEED
- Webbing (depending on the chair shape)
- 12oz hessian or calico
- Staple gun
- Staples
- Upholstery hammer
- Fabric for top cover
- Tape measure
- Scissors
- Pins
- Polyester wadding
- Back tacking card
- Tacks
- Small curved needle
- Slipping thread or any strong thread

The outside back and arms might seem strange places to stuff, but the addition of some polyester wadding helps keep the fabric from rippling and sagging.
The first tutorial that follows is for the traditional hand-sewn finish. If you prefer to use the less time-consuming ply grip, follow the method until step 3, but don't position your fabric, then jump to 'Using ply grip' on page 166.

1 This example is for a tub chair with a curved back. To create the curve for the fabric to follow, add some vertical webs. You don't need to fold the webbing over at the ends, as it's for structure rather than strength. (A fold would also add bulk that could show through the cover.) Here, a line of piping is run around the top of the tub chair.

2 Line the outside arms and back with 12oz hessian or calico if you prefer. This is just a base for the wadding and won't be taking any strain or weight. Fold over and butt the top edge of the hessian against the piping seam allowance – not over it. Staple in place. Here, three pieces of hessian have been used: one for the outside back and two for the outside arms. Stretch down to the base and staple without folding. (You don't want to have a fold line showing through the cover). Fold and staple the remaining edges. If there are any bulky folds of hessian, hammer them flat.

3 For the outside back, measure the top cover with a little excess for positioning and pulling. Cut centre notches at the top and bottom. Also mark the frame. Remember, if there is a pattern it should follow from the inside back and down the outside back (but both running from top to bottom). Pin the outside back in place. Trim back the fabric at the top to about 1.5cm (¾in) and fold under. Pin in place.

4 Cut some polyester wadding. If the back is straight, cut a length of back tacking card. It's best at this point to turn the chair over so that the area you are working on is flat. Fold back the fabric to expose the hessian. Cover the fabric with the polyester and place the card on top of both. Make sure the card butts up tight to the piping. Staple all along the card, starting from the middle and working out.

5 Bring all the layers down and temporary tack the fabric in position on the underside of the back stretcher rail. Turn the fabric under at the sides and pin in place. Make sure there is an even stretch or pull across the fabric.

6 When the fabric is positioned, the top and sides need to be slip stitched. Hide the slipknot between the piping and fabric. Make one stitch in the outside back, then take the thread through the piping and make the next stitch on the inside back, then back through the piping and so on. When the outside back is complete, finish the outside arms in the same way by repeating steps 3 to 6.

7 Take out the temporary tacks and pull the fabric taut. This tub chair has straight legs at the back, so a simple 'V' cut is made and the fabric folded under on either side.

Tub chair piping 1

Outside back and arms 2

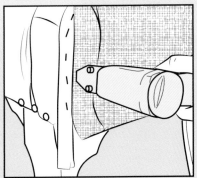

Outside back and arms 5

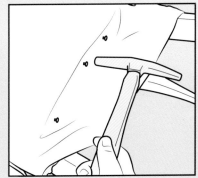

Tub chair piping 2

Outside back and arms 3

Outside back and arms 6

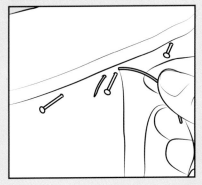

Outside back and arms 1

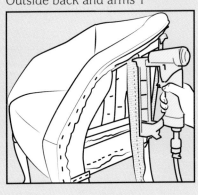

Outside back and arms 4

Outside back and arms 7

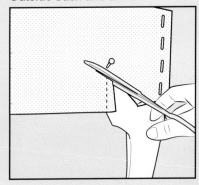

Bringing it all together

Using ply grip

YOU WILL NEED
- Ply grip
- Staple gun
- Staples
- Old scissors
- Polyester wadding
- Hessian or calico
- Tacks
- Upholstery hammer
- Regulator
- Wooden mallet

Having followed the hand-sewn tutorial on page 164, you might opt to finish your chair with ply grip. This makes for a really clean line in a matter of minutes. It also has the benefit of moving around curves, unlike back tacking card.

1 Follow steps 1 and 2 on page 164. Position the ply grip close to the piping. Staple half through the hole and half on the outside of the grip.

2 Fold back the top edge a little way – but not completely.

3 Trim any excess using an old pair of scissors – not your fabric-cutting ones.

4 Lay some polyester wadding over the hessian. Staple in a few places (just enough to hold) and trim back.

5 Now lay the outside back over the poly and trim back the top to about 2cm (¾in) above the ply grip. You can use a couple of tacks on the bottom just to hold the fabric in place, but don't pull tight.

6 Using the flat end of the regulator, tuck the excess fabric under the ply grip. When everything is tucked under, use a wooden mallet (or a fabric-covered mallet) to hammer down the ply grip completely.

Making a fly

YOU WILL NEED
- Fabric
- Sewing machine

If you're running low on fabric supplies or you're on a tight budget, then the addition of a fly could help you out. A fly is essentially a sewn-on piece of fabric that is hidden from view.

1 Measure the amount of fly you will need. For the seat, it will be the point at which the seat and back come together to the bottom rail, plus extra for pulling.

2 Join both pieces of fabric with a plain seam.

3 Fold over the seam allowance and machine again, making a top stitch.

Bottom cloth

You can leave the underside of the chair open, or finish it off with some bottom cloth. Turn the chair over and measure the base plus about 5cm (2in). As always, temporary tack on one side, then pull to the other, and repeat on the remaining two sides. Trim back any excess then turn under and tack. Make any necessary cuts around the legs, and you're done.

Ply grip 1

Ply grip 4

Fly 2

Ply grip 2

Ply grip 5

Fly 3

Ply grip 3

Ply grip 6

Fly: finished item

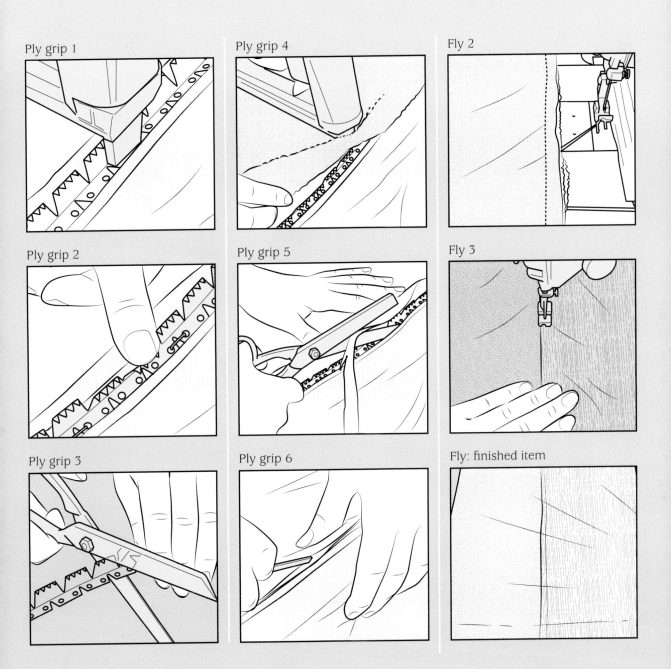

Tufting

There's something amazingly satisfying about tufting – whether it's the traditional deep variety or more contemporary floating buttoning. This tutorial is for deep buttoning a simple foam-filled stool. You can use any type of stuffing, but foam is probably the easiest to work with.

YOU WILL NEED

- Something to button – in this case, a stool
- Foam
- Scissors
- Tailor's chalk
- Drill with circular wood cutter attachment
- Skewers
- Marker pen
- Spray adhesive
- Polyester wadding
- Top cover fabric
- Nylon thread
- Buttons
- Webbing
- Buttoning needle
- Staple gun
- Staples
- Tacks
- Hammer
- Regulator

In this example, the marking out couldn't be simpler. It's a rectangular shape so everything needs to be even and centred. Find the centre lines and play around with some large coloured pins. Stand back and keep checking until you're happy; do what you feel works visually. Measure the average widths and heights for the diamonds. It's also best to make sure there's breathing room around the buttoned area – the distance between the last button and the edge should be bigger than the distance between buttons.

MARKING AND CUTTING THE FOAM

You will need to mark the foam, the fabric and the underside of the stool.

1 Cut the foam so it projects slightly over the stool edges; here, 6cm (2½in) deep foam is used. If you want a really firm edge, wall it with some reconstituted foam. Do not attach to the frame at this point. Mark the centre lines on the top of the foam and the diamonds.

2 The diamonds shown here are 15cm (6in) wide by 22cm (9in) long. The centre lines on the sides of the foam and the sides of the stool are also marked.

3 Drill out the holes right through the foam. Drill a hole in a piece of wood first to use as a guide.

MARKING OUT THE BASE

4 This stool has a hessian base. Mark out the diamond pattern, then transfer it to the underside using skewers and marking with a pen. If your stool has a solid base, mark out the diamond formation and drill holes through the stool that are only large enough for two pieces of twine to pass through.

BRINGING IT ALL TOGETHER

5 Spray glue the foam on top of the stool, making sure to line up with the holes and the marked centre lines.

6 Cover the foam in polyester wadding, over the top and down the sides. With your fingers, tear the wadding over the buttonholes in the foam.

1

3

5

2

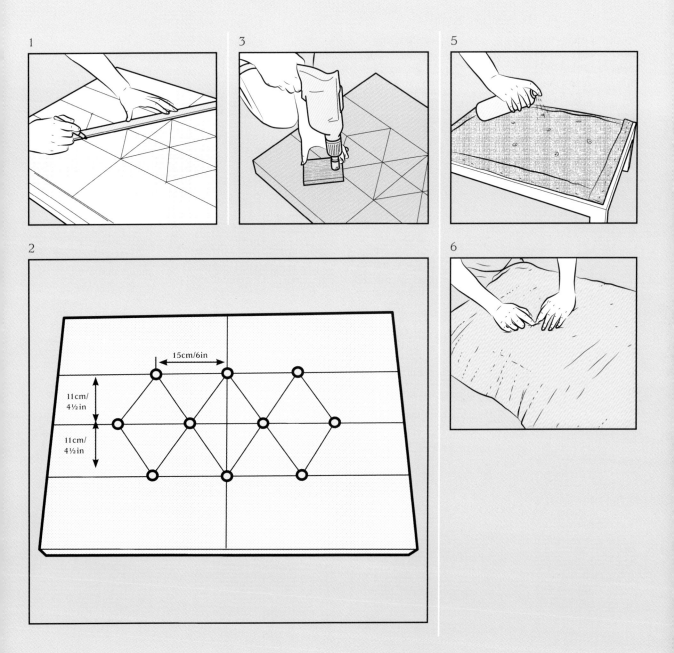

15cm/6in

11cm/
4½in

11cm/
4½in

6

Tufting

MARKING OUT THE FABRIC

7 Mark out the back of the fabric in this order: centre line; horizontal line; height of diamonds; width of diamonds. Draw the diagonal lines to form the diamond shapes.

BUTTONING

8 Cut some nylon thread pieces for as many buttons as you have and cut the same number of square pieces of webbing. Thread some nylon thread through the button and the two loose ends through the eye of the buttoning needle. It's best to start on one line of buttons. Put the buttoning needle through the fabric on the right side on one of your marks.

9 Pull the needle all the way through the hole, pulling the button down into the foam. At this stage don't pull completely down as you want to be able to position the fabric correctly.

10 Fold one of the webbing pieces and tie a slip knot around it. This will hold the button in position. If you have a solid base, use either a tack or a staple.

11 Continue with the buttons on that line, and then do the rest. As your diamonds start to form, begin to work the fabric into neat folds using the flat end of the regulator. This may take some time and you'll probably find yourself moving from button to button. It's easier to work the folds if all your buttons are pulled through to the same depth.

12 Work the outer folds, keeping the rules in mind (see 'Rules for diamonds' opposite). Pull down the buttons to the correct depth and permanently tie off, keeping the webbing in place.

DIAMOND DIMENSIONS

In this example, the buttons will eventually be about 4cm (1½in) deep into the foam. This measurement is pretty average, so stick to it for your first project. When measuring the top fabric you need to take into account this depth measurement for both the width and height of your diamonds. The average allowance for each diamond is 4cm (1½in) in the height and 4.5cm (1¾in) across the width.

The diamond dimensions are:
15cm (6in) wide × 22cm (9in) high.

So the diamond dimensions on the fabric, including the depth of the buttons, are: 19.5cm (7½in) wide × 26cm (10¼in) high.

Add together these measurements for each diamond. Then add to this the distance between the buttons and the frame edge, down the side and extra for pulling. If you have enough fabric you could add 10cm (4in) for pulling to be safe.

MARKING OUT ON A CHAIR

The buttoning must be in proportion and sympathetic to your piece. Lay and pin some calico over the chair to be buttoned. Mark out with coloured pins where you want to position your buttons. Stand back and check the effect. Keep it simple – think about whether your chair will eventually have a large cushion or how high your seat will come up, for example.

RULES FOR DIAMONDS

Shape: visually, it's best to make long diamonds – the height measurement should be more than the width. However, feel free to experiment and try making them square.

Direction: the folds you make should all face down if you are working on a chair. It doesn't matter so much with a stool like the one shown here, but usually the folds should be worked in the same direction. The middle fold on the back of a sofa can face in any direction. The folds to the left and right of the centre need to face outwards.

RESCUE PLANS

Sometimes the buttons will easily fall into place, but other times it might be more difficult. If the folds are bagging a little, you can slip stitch them down. Use a similar coloured thread and remember to tuck any loose thread ends under the fold.

8

10

TIP

If your foam is pretty firm you might want to make slight cuts from the outside edges into the button. This will help the folded fabric slide down into the button smoothly. Fold back your wadding and fabric to reveal the foam. Make a slight cut into the foam about 2.5cm (1in) back from the buttonhole. Bring the wadding down over and push this into the cut. Bring back your fabric and make the fold. (This is not always necessary. Make your fold first and if it is not falling properly then try making the cut.)

9

11

Finished item

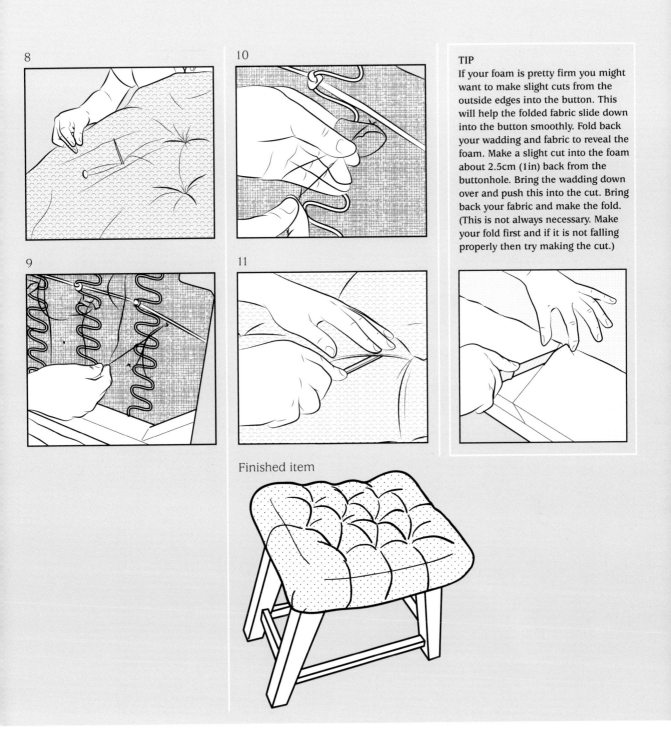

The finishing touches

Traditionally trimmings were used to cover any exposed tacks or staples. You might also plan to add some as extra embellishment or to hide slips with the scissors. Whatever the reason, trimmings are very simple to apply. It doesn't really matter whether you use gimp, braid or double piping. Just be sure it looks good to you and is positioned and attached well.

Attaching trim

YOU WILL NEED
- Trim of your choice, such as gimp
- Scissors
- Hot glue gun
- Coloured gimp pins

1 Turn the end of the trim under and glue any strands together (in this case, gimp was used).

2 Secure the trim to the chair with a coloured gimp pin. It's best to start at the back of the chair where the join will be out of sight.

3 Continue to fix in stages with hot glue. Cover any staples and press the trim tightly against the chair. If you reach any areas where you have to bend around corners, add more gimp pins to secure the trim.

4 Finish by folding both ends of the trim under and gluing so that no stray ends are visible. Hold firmly in place with another gimp pin.

Applying nails

YOU WILL NEED
- Decorative nails
- Tape measure
- Spacer (optional)
- Dressmaking pins (optional)
- Nylon-tipped hammer

1 Work out the spacing you want for the nails. If you want them to sit a certain distance apart, mark the positioning using dressmaking pins.

2 Hammer the nails firmly in.

Applying nail strip

YOU WILL NEED
- Nail strip
- Loose nails that match the strip
- Nylon-tipped hammer

1 Position the nail strip and hammer in a nail at the start.

2 Continue to hammer in nails in the holes, which appear at intervals.

Decorative nails and nail trims

Traditional antique-style nails used to be the only option. Now, however, you can buy an assortment of powder coated, decorative and jewelled varieties. And if that's not enough choice, you could always try painting your own.

Drive the nails home with a nylon-tipped hammer. (If you don't have one you can tie some leather or something else soft over the end of a normal hammer.) In terms of positioning, you'll often see nails sitting shoulder-to-shoulder – close-nailing, as it's referred to. However, creating this look can be quite laborious. If you're impatient, or worried about keeping a perfect line, you can opt for nail strips. If you do prefer to use individual nails, invest in a nail spacer to make your job easier.

Attaching trim 1

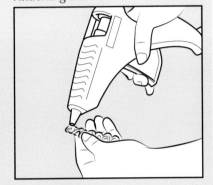

Applying nails 2

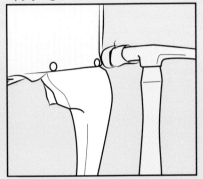

Attaching trim 2

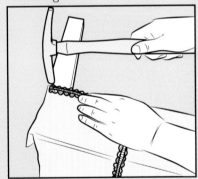

Applying nail strip 2

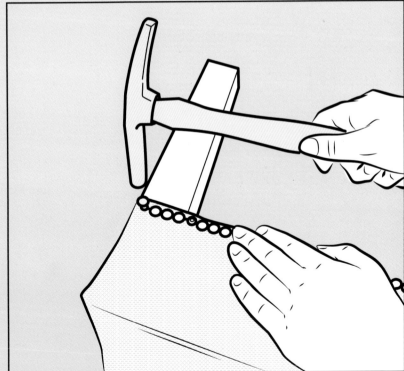

Attaching trim 3

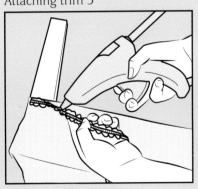

Inca Starzinsky

Inca Starzinsky is a London-based designer specialising in scarves and accessories. A graduate of Central Saint Martins and the Royal College of Art, Inca has worked variously as a graphic designer, printed textile designer, design director and artist. Her background in graphic and textile design contributes to the varied themes evident in her work, such as communication, playfulness and everyday objects. Inca explores the potential of digital printing technology to create photographic reproductions that are not possible with traditional screen printing.

FOR TUTORIALS
Webbing: page 108
Lashing the springs: 122

BEFORE   AFTER

Inca's inspiration for this piece was an imaginary woman, the original owner of the chair when it was new. She decided to create some fabric, digitally printed to make it look like the woman's possessions were still carelessly lying on the chair. The first step was to find the images for the fabric. 'I collected antique items that looked as though they could have belonged to the woman. Some of the items were from my grandmother, including a photo of my grandfather, and other items were borrowed from friends and family. I experimented with the selection and arrangement of the items on the chair, so it would look as though they had just been left there.'

All the antique items were photographed from above at a high resolution. Digital printing is a lot more forgiving of low resolution than a real photographic print, as the printed image 'bleeds' (blurs) a lot on the fabric and is not as sharp. However, Inca wanted to get a look that was as close as possible to the real thing to enhance the *trompe l'oeil* effect. To achieve this, she experimented with hue and saturation settings in Photoshop and sharpened the image in order to get some of the crispness back that is normally lost in fabric prints. She had a sample made before the final print to test the colour and sharpness. Inca explains: 'This can be costly, but it is worth it, as you want to make sure the colours and image quality are as you intended.'

The images of the objects were digitally cut out so that they could be placed onto a flat-coloured background. All the individual pieces of fabric from the chair were measured and a template for each was made in Photoshop, where Inca positioned the individual objects, making sure they were at their original size.

The final files were then sent to the printer, who digitally printed, steamed and washed the fabric. When fabrics are coated in preparation for printing, the fabric is stretched while it dries in order to avoid wrinkling. Some materials stretch a lot, some just a little. After it has been printed, steamed, washed and dried, it will shrink back to its original size; therefore, the print can shrink, depending on the fabric used. A good printer knows the percentage of fabric shrinkage and will stretch the image accordingly before printing to avoid distortion. If not, the shrinkage can be calculated by measuring the test sample against the original image file.

CHAIR STYLE
Victorian bedroom chair.

FABRIC USED
Fabric was designed especially for the chair and was digitally printed onto cotton drill.

ORIGINAL STATE
The fabric was in really bad shape. The springs had dropped and the frame was loose.

CHANGES MADE
The seat was stripped back completely, but the stuffed pad was re-used. The frame was repaired with a combination of dowels, screws and glue.

TIME SPENT
Possibly a week or so of designing, photographing, re-touching and positioning as per the template. About a week's wait for test prints followed by corrections and layout defining, then another week for the fabric to arrive. The upholstery took a couple of days, including frame fixing.

Once the fabric was designed, Inca could turn her attention to the chair. The back was wobbling pretty badly. After ripping away most of the upholstery, it became evident that someone had tried to fix this up before and it was now failing. Inca clamped and dowelled the two back legs to the seat base, and glued and screwed the circular back rest to the leg uprights. She had planned to just tighten up the webbing as it was sagging a little, but on closer inspection, she could see that the springs had broken through the hessian and were working their way up through the stuffing. She removed the stuffed seat pad and put it to one side, then re-webbed, sprung, and lashed the seat and added another layer of hessian. She also added some more fibre to the middle and a little to the sides as the seat had sunk, which was probably due to the webbing being loose and hanging down under the chair. She re-positioned the stuffed pad and stapled it in place. Luckily the hessian was still in good shape and there was plenty to staple into. Inca regulated the fibre on top of the pad, covered it with a layer of cotton felt and then lined it with calico. This was followed with two layers of polyester, then the top cover. The back of the chair had sunk a little, so Inca firmed it up by webbing the back. She also added another layer of cotton felt and some polyester before fixing the top cover.

Matching up the pieces of fabric was not very difficult. Inca had been pretty precise and once the piping was made, it all sat together perfectly. The fabric is actually white, it is the print that is black; this meant that whenever a needle touched the fabric, some of the black print came away and exposed the white. 'Luckily this didn't happen on any visible areas! If any white dots had appeared, I would have tested a spare fabric piece with some Dylon. I know that it is tempting to reach for the black marker or biro, but don't do this! Black ink often looks purple and really stands out in different light.' The chair was then finished with double piping and a couple of upholstery nails at the back.

Every vintage item has its own story. Mostly, we have no idea what this story is, we can only imagine. I wanted to create the character of a woman who lived 100 years ago and left some of her items lying on the chair while getting ready. She no longer lives, but through the presence of her possessions, she is almost in the room, like a ghost

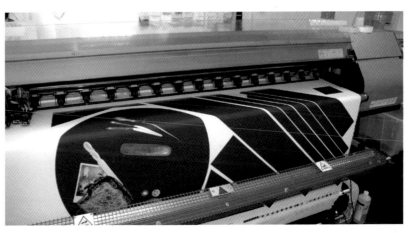

SECTION 4
Resources

Birds n Bees fabric
by Timorous Beasties.

Glossary

BANQUETTE
Long upholstered, bench-like seating usually built up against a wall. Common in bars and restaurants.

BIAS CUT
'The bias' is a 45-degree cut made across the warp and weft threads of fabric. Piping is usually cut on the bias making it more flexible and easier to manipulate.

BLIND STITCH
A stitch used in traditional upholstery to create a firm edge. The loops of twine made within the upholstery hold the stuffing close and compact to the edge. Generally, the more blind stitches the firmer and higher the edge.

BOTTOM CLOTH
A cloth, normally black or brown, that attaches to the underside of a chair hiding the webbing and springs from view. It's unlikely you'll ever see the bottom cloth and it's not absolutely necessary to have it, but using it gives a professional finish.

BOX CUSHION
Also known as a bordered cushion, this is a cushion with a sewn bordered edge in the shape of a box. Some are zipped and others are hand sewn together. Fillings range from foam to feathers.

BRAID
A flat type of trimming. Generally used as a decorative edge and to cover exposed tacks or staples.

BRIDLE TIES
Overlapping looped twine sewn through hessian. Stuffing is then positioned under each loop.

CAMPAIGN CHAIR
A mid nineteenth-century chair that can be transported by folding.

CAPPED ON, OR 'CAP ON'
Pre-sewn fabric sections that just slip into position on furniture. They are then permanently stapled or tacked in place.

CHAISE LONGUE
French term for an upholstered day bed. A chair for reclining.

CLOSE NAILING
Decorative nailing set side by side.

COIR
The treated husk of a coconut. It is cleaned, curled and sometimes dyed. Its natural colour is ginger. Coir is quite coarse and strong and so is generally used as a first stuffing.

CUTTING PLAN
A drawn plan of how each panel (piece of fabric) will be cut from a length of fabric.

DEEP BUTTONING
Deep-set buttons usually positioned in a diamond formation. The buttons are pulled into the upholstery using twine and the loose fabric manipulated into folds between each button.

DROP-IN SEAT
A seat that can be detached from the frame and upholstered separately. Common on simple dining chairs.

FLY
An unseen piece of fabric sewn to the top cover. This fabric lengthens the top cover so that it can be pulled down to the rails. The fly is usually made from cheaper fabric than the top fabric. The fly fabric does, however, need to be strong. It is sewn together with a plain stitch, folded over, then top stitched.

FLOATING BUTTONS (FLOAT BUTTONING)
Buttons held to a cushion or upholstery using twine. Unlike deep buttoning, the buttons 'float' or make a small indent in the cover.

FRINGE
A style of decorative trimming. Usually a simple braid at the top with a hanging fringe.

GIMP
A woven decorative trimming. Often looped in appearance, sometimes with wire running through it.

GIMP PINS
Small coloured tacks for keeping gimp in place. They can also be used in areas where a tack would be too large. Can also be used as a visible fixing, for an outside back for example.

HIDE
The treated skin of animals such as cows, goats and pigs for use in upholstery.

JUTE
A vegetable fibre spun into strong threads. It is used to make webbing, hessian, sacking and scrim.

Interior designer Marie Olsson Nylander. Photography by Sara Svenningrud.

LAID CORD
A thick cord made from flax with little twist, therefore unlikely to stretch. Used for lashing springs into position.

LASHING
The tying and knotting of springs together and to the chair frame using laid cord.

NAP
The raised surface of fabric, especially velvet. If you run your hand in the direction of the nap it is smooth. Run against and it is rough. The nap should run down a chair, i.e. from the top of the back or top of the arm to the seat.

NOTCH
A 'V' cut in fabric, usually used to mark a centre point or as a marker for pieces of fabric.

PINCERS
A tool with a crab-like head. A type of plier used to remove tacks and staples from furniture frames.

PIPING
Welt cord covered in a specific fabric for a project. Single piping is used for a strong seam or as a design detail. Double piping is used as a trimming in the same way as gimp or braid. Piping is attached to furniture with hot glue and gimp pins.

PLATFORM
An area on the seat of a chair supporting a cushion. Usually covered in a specific platform lining.

REGULATING
The movement of fibre with a regulator to create an even, knot-free stuffing.

REGULATOR
A tool with one sharp and one flat end. Used to regulate fibre. It is also useful in making folds for corners, pleats and deep buttoning.

RIPPING DOWN
The removal of old upholstery coverings, tacks and staples.

SEAM ALLOWANCE
The area between the edge of fabric and the stitched line.

SERPENTINE SPRING
A looped or zigzigged spring. Held to a chair frame with clips.

SHOW WOOD
Wooden part of the chair frame that stays exposed once the upholstery is completed. The show wood is often finished with varnish, wax or paint.

SKEWERS
Long pin with a circular end. Hold fabric temporarily in place where a tack or staple can't be used.

SPRING UNIT
A system of cone springs brought together in a unit.

STITCHED EDGE
A firm edge of upholstery made with traditional materials such as horse hair or coir. The stuffing is covered in hessian or scrim. A combination of blind and top stitching creates the firm edge.

TEASING
The pulling apart of lumpy fibres to make stuffing more even.

TRESTLE
Two frames joined by a piece of wood. Two trestles are used in upholstery with or without a table top.

TUB CHAIR
Chair with a curved inside.

WARP
Threads that run from top to bottom on a length of fabric.

WEBBING
Strong woven strips used to support springs and subsequent layers of stuffing. Found on the underside of a chair or sofa. Traditionally made from jute but also made from rubber in modern furniture.

WEFT
Threads that run from side to side on a length of fabric.

WELT
Another name for the cord used to make piping.

Grane sofa by BDDW.

Useful websites

MAGAZINES

American Craft Council
www.craftcouncil.org/magazine

Elle Decor
www.elledecor.com

Selvedge Magazine
www.selvedge.org

Surface Design Journal
surfacedesign.org

Upholstery Journal
upholsteryjournalmag.com

BLOGS

Apartment Therapy
www.apartmenttherapy.com

The Art of Doing Stuff
www.theartofdoingstuff.com

Chair Smith
chairsmith.blogspot.co.uk

decor8
decor8blog.com

Design Milk
design-milk.com

Design*Sponge
www.designsponge.com

Ellie Tennant
ellietennant.com/blog

The London Chair Collective
blog.thelondonchaircollective.com

Sight Unseen
www.sightunseen.com

UPHOLSTERERS

Emily Farncombe
www.emilyfarncombe.co.uk

Relovestuff
www.relovestuff.co.uk

Sarah Hill
www.no5studios.com

Spruce
spruceaustin.com

FURNITURE SUPPLIERS

Chase and Sorensen
www.chaseandsorensen.com

Osi Modern
www.osimodern.com

Skandinavian Vintage
skandinavianvintage.co.uk

Hopper and Space
www.hopperandspace.com

Knoll
www.knoll.com

Ercol
www.ercol.com

Twentytwentyone
www.twentytwentyone.com

Vitra
www.vitra.com/en-gb

DIGITAL FABRIC PRINTERS

Cameron Gilmartin
www.camerongilmartin.co.uk

Centre for Advanced Textiles
www.catdigital.co.uk

R A Smarts
www.rasmart.co.uk

Spoonflower
www.spoonflower.com

UPHOLSTERY SUPPLIERS

C. S. Osborne & Co.
www.csosborne.com

Gary's Upholstery Products LLC
www.garysupholstery.com

Heico Fastners
www.heico-fasteners.co.uk

J A Milton Upholstery Supplies Ltd
www.jamiltonupholstery.co.uk

Martins Upholstery Suppliers Ltd
www.martinsupholstery.co.uk

Perfect fit
www.perfectfit.com

VV Rouleaux
www.vvrouleaux.com

FABRIC SUPPLIERS & DESIGNERS

Andrew Martin
www.andrewmartin.co.uk

Bute
www.butefabrics.com

Camira
www.camirafabrics.com

Celia Birtwell
www.celiabirtwell.com

Cloud 9 Fabrics
www.cloud9fabrics.com

Fabric.com
www.fabric.com

House of Hackney
www.houseofhackney.com

Ian Mankin
www.ianmankin.co.uk

Kvadrat
www.kvadrat.dk

Liberty
www.liberty.co.uk

St Judes
www.stjudesfabrics.co.uk

Timorous Beasties
www.timorousbeasties.com

Arden fabric designed by Melissa White for Zoffany.

Index

Contributors

CASE STUDIES

Eleanor Young
www.funmakesgood.co.uk

Hayley Beham
dailyhaley.wordpress.com

Inca Starzinsky
www.incastarzinsky.com

Jude Dennis
www.thelondonchaircollective.com/jude-dennis.html

Kristin Jackson
thehuntedinterior.blogspot.co.uk

Marianne Songbird
www.songbirdblog.com

Patrick Feist
pmfeist.com

Sarah Whyberd
sarahwhyberd.tumblr.com

OTHER CONTRIBUTORS

BDDW
bddw.com
Founded by Tyler Hays, BDDW is a small furniture company dedicated to the creation of well-crafted, timeless designs. Its furniture is made from select domestic hardwoods and is traditionally joined. BDDW is based in New York.

Camilla Hounsell Halvorsen
www.camillahounsellhalvorsen.com
Camilla achieved her Master's degree in interior architecture and furniture design at Oslo National Academy of the Arts in 2011, with a special interest in sustainability. A prototype of her Drops Pouf design is part of the permanent collection of the Art Museum in Bergen, Norway. She sells a variety of handmade products online, ranging from furniture to earrings.

Claire-Anne O'Brien
www.claireanneobrien.com
Originally from Ireland, Claire-Anne is a textile designer based in London. After graduating from Central Saint Martins in 2006 with a BA in Textiles, she went on to gain an MA in Knitted Textiles at the Royal College of Art in 2010. In 2011 she received the Future Makers Award from the Crafts Council of Ireland. With a sculptural approach to textiles, Claire-Anne explores form, construction and scale through the unique properties of knitted fabrics.

Florrie + Bill
www.florrieandbill.com
Florrie + Bill sell lovingly restored retro and vintage furniture, as well as offering bespoke upholstery services. The company is based in Leicestershire, UK.

Flourish and Blume
flourishandblume.blogspot.com
Laura McEwan and Katie Blume of Flourish and Blume are on a mission to save chairs. They salvage mid-century furniture found in their hometown of Lismore, Australia and upholster and restore it using local, handmade and sustainable materials and fabrics wherever possible.

GUBI
www.gubi.dk
Danish furniture company GUBI was founded in 1967 by Gubi and Lisbeth Olsen. It produces an eclectic range of furniture, including reproductions of 'forgotten icons' from the 1930s through to the 1970s. As well as these design classics, GUBI also collaborates with emerging designers on a range of exciting new pieces.

Ink & Spindle
inkandspindle.com
Ink & Spindle is a boutique textile studio located in Melbourne, Australia. It is owned by designers Lara Cameron and Tegan Rose, who design and screen-print all their textiles by hand in an ethical and sustainable manner. Their designs are largely inspired by Australia's native flora and fauna.

Jesse Breytenbach
jezzeblog.blogspot.com
Jesse Breytenbach is a freelance illustrator and printmaker based in Cape Town, South Africa. Her textiles are produced using locally sourced fabrics and hand-printing techniques.

Like That One
www.likethatone.com
The aim of Like That One is to bring some fun, some DIY spirit and some vintage cool to Singapore. The company restores and re-purposes vintage Singapore furniture, creating a sense of rootedness in a city that prizes the new.

Lucy Davidson
peasandneedles.blogspot.com
Lucy is a UK-based illustrator, graphic designer and needleworker working with both print and textiles.

MYK
myk-berlin.com
MYK was established in 2009 by fashion designer Myra Klose. The company produces soft furnishings and furniture, all of which are handcrafted in Germany.

Shelly Miller Leer
www.modhomeec.com
After nearly twenty years of owning her own custom upholstery studio, Shelly Miller Leer transitioned her business into a fully dedicated teaching program. Geared towards avid DIY-ers, she offers a wide variety of upholstery, sewing and furniture building classes in her Indianapolis SoBro (South Broad Ripple) studio. She has been a featured writer for Curbly.com and a contributor to ApartmentTherapy Chicago, as well as being featured in other well known DIY blogs, magazines and books. She writes a weekly DIY column for *The Indianapolis Star* and Indystar.com.

Skinny laMinx
skinnylaminx.com
Skinny laMinx is the design label of the self-taught illustrator and designer Heather Moore. Based in Cape Town, South Africa, Heather's work is inspired by Scandinavian designs and mid-century style. She produces a successful range of screen-printed fabrics, as well as selling sewn items, papergoods and decorations.

Tango & James
tangoandjames.blogspot.com
Founded by fashion and interior designer Lisa Barrett, Tango & James offers a collection of unique creations, including fabrics, jewellery, handbags and homewares, as well as restored furniture. Lisa lives in Canberra, Australia.

Tortie Hoare
www.tortiehoare.co.uk
Designer Tortie Hoare produces handmade furniture that is ergonomic, durable and aesthetically pleasing. She combines old methods with new ways of thinking to create unique and contemporary pieces.

Urban Upholstery
www.urbanupholstery.com
Established in 2007 by Andrea Simonutti and Patrizia Sottile, Urban Upholstery is a London-based company that recycles existing furniture, as well as creating new pieces. It provides consultation, design, restoration and upholstery services to a wide variety of clients, ranging from individuals and businesses to furniture designers and collectors.

Wild Chairy
www.wildchairy.com
Andrea Mihalik is the artist behind Wild Chairy. Her hand-crafted designs combine traditional techniques, eco-friendly materials and bold contemporary fabrics to create one-of-a-kind pieces of functional art. Also an award-winning photojournalist, Andrea is based in New Jersey.

Acknowledgements

Thank you firstly to my mum Diane. I know my need for a rural retreat is always there and much love, support and 'world to rights' banter on offer at the kitchen table. Thank you to Matthias, my husband. Along with the occasional supportive words, you know an Indian take-away is the way to keep stress levels low. It's been a challenging year of personal projects and I'm always amazed by your level-headed calm in every fraught moment.

To all my friends who remained consistently excited by the prospect of me writing a book – followed by questions of why, months on, I was still writing a book – your optimism and capacity for listening is immense. Special thanks to Jack, for being Jack. And of course to Alex, Camilla, Inca, Marion and Dom. Team DRY, Martin, Liz and Ruth, and not forgetting Charlotte. Yet more special thanks and gratitude to Nat, for making me furniture and the occasional spritzers with red wine chasers. And Rob, one day you'll have the Stanton chaise…

My turn around in career could not have been possible without Malcolm, Alex, Matt, Andy and all the technicians on the upholstery and finishing courses at the London Met. Their commitment to teaching to the highest of standards and sharing invaluable knowledge about the insides and outsides of chairs is unparalleled. Malcolm, your skill as an upholsterer is exceptional and your knowledge of cruising – off the scale. Long may the course and others like it continue.

Thank you to Jane, Isheeta, Jen, Emily and the rest of the team at RotoVision. You have executed the book with great skill and professionalism. And your patience, especially in the closing stages, has been amazing. Thank you to the many contributors of great upholstery projects and providers of images that have really brought life to the book. Special thanks to Michael Wicks for the opening spreads of tools and to Joe Gascoigne for mine and various chair portraits. And thanks to Peters & Zabransky for working tirelessly through the many illustrations.

I'm now looking forward to actually being in the workshop with Jude, Esther, Gail, Iain, and Debbie, eating pickled eggs in crisps and drinking beer tea, and wine – in that order. Punctuated, of course with the odd bit of upholstery.

Last of all I'd like to dedicate the book to Chino and Roxy. You have both kept me in the real world (or your version of it) of eating, drinking and what seems like endless sleeping.